ELLEN CONSTANCE NIGHTINGALE

A LIFE

Frontispiece. *E. Constance Nightingale, Headmistress, The Mount School, York, 1940–8. (Artist: Richard Naish. Photo: Courtesy The Mount School, York)*

About the artist: Richard Naish, New English Art Club, 1912–88; Oxford Society from 1948; York School of Art, Royal College of Art, 1932–4; Ruskin School, Oxford, 1934.

ELLEN CONSTANCE NIGHTINGALE

A LIFE

BY

JOHN GRIFFITHS PEDLEY

Copyright © 2021 by John Griffiths Pedley

All rights reserved. No part of this book may be reproduced or transmitted in any form or by any means whatsoever without express written permission from the author, except in the case of brief quotations embodied in critical articles and reviews. Please refer all pertinent questions to the author.

First published 2022 by GnatBooks.

Cover portrait by Richard Naish.

This book was edited and designed by Michael Gnat.

ISBN 978-0-578-35132-2   paperback

The author has no responsibility for the persistence or accuracy of URLs for external or third-party Internet websites referred to in this publication and does not guarantee that any content on such websites is, or will remain, accurate or appropriate.

CONTENTS

List of Illustrations		vii
Acknowledgements		ix
1	SETTING THE STAGE	*page* 1
2	MANCHESTER: THE OPENING WORLD	11
3	BEYOND BRITAIN: PARIS AND CONSTANTINOPLE	21
4	ALEXIS ALADIN	29
5	DR. WILLIAMS' SCHOOL, DOLGELLAU	53
6	THE MOUNT SCHOOL, YORK	81
7	WALES AGAIN: THE RETIREMENT YEARS	105
Select Bibliography		123
Index		125

ILLUSTRATIONS

	E. Constance Nightingale, Headmistress, The Mount School, York, 1940–8	*frontis.*
1.1	42 St. Matthew Street, Burnley: Connie Nightingale's home during her school days	9
2.1	Ashburne Hall, University of Manchester, where Connie Nightingale lived as an undergraduate	15
2.2	Phoebe Sheavyn, Warden of Ashburne Hall and Connie Nightingale's mentor	17
3.1	Ronald Burrows, Connie Nightingale's Professor of Greek at Manchester University	22
3.2	Ronald Burrows at his holiday cottage in North Wales	23
4.1	A raffish Alexis Feodorovich Aladin in Saint Petersburg, 1906	31
4.2	Alexis Aladin with Vladimir Dmitrievich Nabokov in 1906, members of the First Russian Duma	33
4.3	Alexis Aladin in social attire, 1916	35
4.4	Alexis Aladin in British army uniform, 1920	37
4.5	Sir David Russell	39
5.1	Dr. Williams' School in the 1930s	56
5.2	Connie Nightingale, Headmistress, 1924–40	57
5.3	Tremhyfryd and hockey field	59
5.4	Connie Nightingale on the steps of Tremhyfryd	61
5.5	Connie Nightingale and Alexis Jr. shortly after his arrival in Dolgellau	63

5.6	Dr. Williams' School, new hall and library, 1930s	65
6.1	School House, The Mount School, York, 2020	83
6.2	Connie Nightingale as Headmistress of The Mount School, York, 1940–8, portrait head	87
6.3	Alexis Jr. as a teenager	89
6.4	Connie Nightingale with Kathleen Carrick Smith, the new Headmistress of The Mount, in 1948	102
7.1	Ty Newydd, Connie Nightingale's house on the lower slopes of Cader Idris, 1930s	107
7.2	Ty Newydd in a recent photograph, with outbuildings converted by a subsequent owner	111
7.3	Connie Nightingale and grandniece Lucy Nightingale in Scarborough in 1964	121
	The Mount School library: bay, table, and chairs and the tablet recording the Old Girls Association's gift to the library in honour of Connie Nightingale, 1968	122

ACKNOWLEDGEMENTS

Many friends, colleagues, and family members have helped in the writing of this book, and I thank them all. The project began as an attempt to outline the history of a small industrial town in the North of England over the past century or so: its growth, periods of prosperity, and precipitous decline. This town is Burnley, a cotton town in Northeast Lancashire nestled up against the Pennine hills, where my family lived and worked for several generations, and which I wanted to describe through the family's experiences. When I began to sketch out these ups and downs, it soon became clear that one family member was preeminent for capacity for hard work, intellectual range, energy, desire (and ability) to contribute to the public good, and concern for the betterment of women's lives, not least the education of girls; and this at a time when women's roles in public life were restricted, for the most part, to teaching and nursing. That person is Connie Nightingale, sister of Tom Nightingale, my mother's brother-in-law, and hence my aunt by marriage.

The book could not have been written without access to the archival resources of several institutions. The staff of Burnley Public Library set me on the right track; amongst them I thank particularly Catherine Fenton and Kim Dean. In Manchester, Sheila Griffiths, archivist of Ashburne Hall, gave generously of her time and knowledge, and James Peters, archivist at the University of Manchester Library, confirmed details of Connie Nightingale's academic career. The curators, archivists, and staff at the John Rylands Library, a division of the University of Manchester Library, helped unstintingly over several years in the perusal of the Aladin Papers and the provision of photographs. I acknowledge especially the help of Fran Baker, archivist, in the initial stages of the work; and more recently that of Kate Miller, Reader Services Coordinator, and of Dr. Janette Martin, Modern History Archivist (Special Collections) and curator responsible for the Alexis Aladin Papers. At the Record Office for Leicestershire, Leicester and Rutland, Jess Jenkins answered my questions promptly and helpfully.

At the Dolgellau Records Office I received valuable assistance from Gethin Jones, Elaine Roberts, and Merfyn Wyn Tomos, Meirionnydd Archivist (now retired), who went out of his way to find photographs and whose important book *"Honour before Honours": The DWS Story* (Bala, 2009) I have consulted frequently. Anna Z. Skarżyńska, Senior Archivist, Ceredigion Archives, Aberystwyth and Meirionnydd Archivist, Dolgellau, kindly provided an edited copy of the DWS catalogue and was a constant source of good advice and encouragement. At the University of York's Borthwick Institute for Archives, the academic unit responsible for the records of The Mount School, Graham Hughes, Nick Melia, and Sally Kent were reliable helpers, and at The Mount School itself Vanessa Charters offered indispensable assistance, not least in acquiring photographs of the portrait of Connie Nightingale. At the Special Collections Division of the University of St. Andrews Library Anabel Farrell informed me quickly of the range of correspondence between Sir David Russell and Connie Nightingale and arranged for the scanning of more than 350 letters between the two, thus sparing me the long journey to Scotland. Sarah Rodriguez, Sean Rippington, and Britta Funck-Januschke also contributed in their different ways.

Jennie Forrester showed great enthusiasm for this project from our very first email encounter, pointing me to the wealth of information about Dr. Williams' School on the website of the Old Girls Association, correcting several errors in earlier versions of the book, and introducing me to Merfyn Wyn Tomos. I am very grateful to her. Through Jennie's agency Megan Huggins put me in direct touch with Morris Higham, the current owner of Ty Newydd, Connie's cottage at the foot of Cader Idris; Morris Higham kindly sent me the current photograph of the cottage published here, with further information about developments to and near the site. An old family friend in Burnley, Ken Spencer, well-known ornithologist, local historian, and environmentalist, shed much light on ECN's early life and schooling. Simon Howe, one of Connie's great-nephews, was able to find, amidst the cascades of paper in his office, a copy of Connie's sister Alice's memoir, which cast their mother in a new light. Lucy Nightingale Chamberlain capped her continuing interest in the project by contributing the photograph of Connie and herself as a child, a photo taken by my cousin and boyhood sidekick, Barry, her father.

Designed and edited by Michael Gnat the book has been greatly improved by his sharp eye, his organisational know-how, and his telling turn of phrase. It has been a pleasure to work with him.

My most heartfelt gratitude is reserved for my wife, Mary: gratitude, and admiration, for her editorial skills, her intellect, her wit, her smile, her ability to shake me out of the doldrums. My companion now for more than fifty years, she has been with me and this project every step of the way, and it would not have been completed without her.

CHAPTER

1

SETTING THE STAGE

Ellen Constance ("Connie") Nightingale (1892–1967) was born in Burnley, Lancashire, a cotton town at the end of a string of similar towns reaching northeastwards from Manchester to the Pennine hills. The high moors where the Brontë sisters lived are within walking distance to the east, with Top Withens, the derelict farmhouse often identified as the inspiration for Emily Brontë's Wuthering Heights, just beyond the horizon. To the west Pendle Hill – famous for the witches who lived in the forest around its southern slopes, many of them brought to trial and hanged at Lancaster in 1612 – rises up, like a flat-backed whale, to an elevation of some two thousand feet. Pendle is famous too for the visit forty years later, in the early days of the Quaker movement, of George Fox (1624–91). Climbing to the summit – "with difficulty," as he admitted – he experienced a vision. Seeing the coast of Lancashire in the distance, he went on, "the Lord let me see in what places he had a great people to be gathered."[1]

Burnley

Initially, farming (smallholdings) and handloom weaving encouraged by a damp climate provided a living for many. Two factors account for the climate. Clouds running up against the Pennine hills release plenty of rain,

---

1. George Fox, *A Journal or Historical Account of the Life, Travels, Sufferings, . . .*, 3rd ed. (London: Richardson & Clark, 1765), p. 66.

and when handloom weaving gave way to power weaving, the rivers Brun and Calder provided the water to power the machinery in the sheds and foundries. Second, the geological base of the area is millstone grit, a tough siliceous rock, on which sits a thick clayey earth topped by coarse grasses, bogs, and moorland. This effectively slows the dispersal of surface water, encouraging the damp.

By the early seventeenth century Burnley had developed from a small group of mediaeval farms centred on the Brun and the Calder into a flourishing market town with a central church and a grammar school, the school where Jonas (later Sir Jonas) Moore, the famous seventeenth-century mathematician and surveyor, got his start. By the 1750s Burnley had added manufacturing to its activities. Initially, workshops of weavers used simple textile machines put together by carpenters and blacksmiths to produce high-quality cloth – linen, fustian, and worsted. Over time the small handloom workshops gave way to weaving sheds – mills which towards the end of the century worked less and less with wool and more and more with cotton. Shortly, cotton goods became their major product.

With the introduction of power looms in the mid-nineteenth century the number of mills, foundries, and ironworks which produced the required machinery increased rapidly. Coal pits and collieries to feed the furnaces were opened. These industries benefitted greatly from the Leeds and Liverpool Canal (built ca. 1800). No longer was it necessary to rely on horses and wagons laden with raw cotton slogging up the valleys from Liverpool and Manchester and returning to the docks with cotton goods and coal for export. New mills were sited near the canal for ease of transport and access to the water needed for their boilers. A further boost came ca. 1850 when the expanding railway system reached the town. The American Civil War (1861–5) brought embargoes on cotton and tough times for the town, but the rally after the war was so robust that by 1885 Burnley was building more looms than any other town in England. A population of barely 4,000 in 1800 had grown to almost 87,000. The noise and grime of machinery, as well as the fresh air of Pendle Hill and the moors, were amongst Connie Nightingale's early experiences.

From the turn of the century to the outbreak of World War I (1914) was the period of the town's greatest prosperity. Considered the centre of cotton manufacturing in Britain, the town boasted upwards of a hundred spinning and weaving mills. One of the more successful firms, B. Thornber and Sons' "spinning and weaving complex," was thought to be the largest in the world, working 100,000 spindles and 2,500 looms.[2] But a slow decline set in, marked by catastrophic losses of young men in the war (more than four thousand Burnley men killed, not to mention the maimed) and the recession of the 1930s which brought large-scale unemployment and social disruption to the town – a strike of cotton workers in 1932 required the intervention of mounted police from Manchester.

After World War II (1939–45) the complacency of mill owners in the face of foreign competition only accelerated the decline. Many had amassed fortunes and refused to believe that changes in equipment or organisation were needed. The erosion of the industry was accelerated by Prime Minister (1957–63) Harold Macmillan's government. Well intentioned though the Cotton Industry Act of 1959 was, in practice it resulted in the demolition of looms with little or no modernization, followed by mill closures and unemployment.

Following this collapse cotton has almost disappeared from the local economy, leaving the town a dim echo of its old self. The reduction in cotton manufacturing was followed by its Corporation's ill-considered destruction of hundreds of houses, the magnificent market hall, the cattle market, and the Odeon cinema (a 1930s modernist landmark) to make way for a dismal new market hall, high-rise blocks of flats ("concrete jungles"), and office blocks. The deterioration of the town continued in the 1980s, hastened by Margaret Thatcher's brutal policies. A population of about 105,000 in Connie Nightingale's time has shrunk to some 75,000, there are 50,000 fewer jobs now than there were a century ago,[3] and the town centre, once full of activity, is somnolent.

2. Frank Thistlethwaite, *A Lancashire Family Inheritance* (Cambridge: F. Thistlethwaite, 1996), 37.
3. BBC World News, November 2, 2018.

The Family

Connie (b. February 14, 1892) was the third of the six children of Thomas and Annie Nightingale who surived to adulthood.[4] There were four other girls, two older (Edith and Beth) and two younger (Alice and Kathleen), and one boy, Thomas, her junior by four years. Little is known of Annie Nightingale's (née Clitheroe)[5] background except that she was not a Burnley girl, a circumstance often held against her by family members, and was the daughter, perhaps illegitimate, of a builder named Tullis, from Preston, member of a family with Scottish forebears. Connie makes occasional reference to her Scottish roots and her affection for Scotland in her correspondence with David (later Sir David) Russell.

Much more is known about Connie's father, Thomas.[6] The Nightingale family traced its nineteenth-century origins to the village of Tockholes near Blackburn, a part of Lancashire known for its independent spirit, commitment to religious freedom and nonconformist principles, and, politically, its loyalty to Parliament during the Civil War (1642–51) and the Protectorate (1653–9). In this environment the Nightingales prospered, playing an active role in a community of smallholders working the land and hand-loom weaving. Despite the familiarities of rural life, Thomas's father, William (Connie's grandfather) had joined his elder brother, another Thomas, in leaving the world of husbandry for a new and quite different life. Thomas had become the first agent of the Prudential Assurance Company in East Lancashire. When the agency grew more rapidly than he had anticipated, in 1855 he invited William, though only 23 years of age, to join him. Along with other mutually beneficial institutions of the time (the Mechanics Institutes, Building Societies, and the Co-operative movement, for instance), life insurance companies were vehicles of social solidarity, self-improvement, and the cultural optimism in which both brothers believed.

After Thomas's death in 1859, William was the only representative of the Prudential in an area reaching northeastwards from Blackburn to Skipton and Keighley. To be closer to the centre of this large area William and

---

4. Florence, twin sister to Beth, died in 1895. Dora, Alice's twin, died in 1904.
5. Email message from Catherine Fenton, Burnley Library 1-23-2016.
6. Thistlethwaite, pp. 93–125.

his wife and small child had moved in 1855 to Burnley, where, true to their nonconformist upbringing, the family had immediately joined Salem Congregational Church. As the work piled up, William was busier than ever, frequently travelling to clients far away. Yet he found time for relaxation at home, keeping an allotment for vegetables and chickens, and in later, more prosperous times owning a greenhouse where his interest in plant varieties flourished. Though well known for generosity to his clients, he was said to have been tyrannical with his children, only – for instance – letting his daughters marry if their spouses gave him a weekly stipend! His wife, Elizabeth ("Betty"), Connie's grandmother, was a Robinson of the family which had worked Slade Farm near Padiham for years; the child of a farming family she had been educated in her earliest years at a dame school – a small school run by an older woman out of her own home. She and William had nine surviving children, of whom the fourth, born in 1861, was Thomas, Connie's father.

Little is known of Thomas's early life. In his twenties he emerges as a gregarious young man, a regular at chapel services and social evenings where his liking for music and drama was soon in evidence. Also an enterprising businessman, he formed a partnership with James Leslie, the two of them launching the firm of Leslie and Nightingale, Builders, Contractors, Quarry Masters, and Builders' Merchants. Thanks to the rapid expansion of the cotton industry in the last quarter of the century, the growth of Burnley's population, and the consequent demand for new housing, they were able to acquire quarries, employ master masons, and complete several large-scale projects. With the town growing in all directions, some families were looking for properties uphill on the south side of town where there was open ground, less smoke, and more fresh air. It was here that Leslie and Nightingale concentrated their efforts building terrace after terrace of sturdy stone-built dwellings, some smaller for working-class families, others larger for the more affluent. Thomas built a particularly fine house for his brother-in-law, Sharp Thornber. Standing at the top end of a terrace, Green Hill Terrace, well located close to a large tract of land (thirteen acres, bequeathed to the town by Alderman J. H. Scott for the development of a public park) and completed in 1893, the house comprised entrance hall, sitting room, dining room, kitchen, scullery, four bedrooms, a maid's room, and a box (storage) room. For a family of the emerging middle class, it had a touch of luxury about it.[7]

In the same year and the same area Leslie and Nightingale completed another elegant terrace of houses, Beech Grove Terrace, into which they soon moved their own families, the Nightingales to No. 163 Coal Clough Lane (Connie aged 1), the Leslies to No. 165;[8] down the road, not a stone's throw away, was Colonel W. J. Frampton in Coal Clough House. The Nightingale house was well suited to the growing family (Thomas and Annie and their four daughters, Edith, Elizabeth, Florence, and Connie), on the edge of town with a garden, greenhouses, and an orchard leading down to a stream. By now prosperous with a booming business, Thomas busied himself, amongst other responsibilities, with the workhorses at the quarries, and as a hobby kept a kennel of dogs for breeding and showing. Shortly afterwards, when his elder brother Luther returned from a failed enterprise in Brazil, their imperious father, William, demanded that Thomas make Luther a partner in the firm and take a younger brother, William, also into the business. What the terms of the agreement were we do not know, but in 1896 at any rate Thomas's and Luther's and James Leslie's families all were living side by side on Beech Grove Terrace.[9] Nor do we know why in the following year the partnership "heretofore subsisting between us the undersigned James Leslie, Thomas Nightingale and Luther Nightingale" was dissolved,[10] and can only surmise that James Leslie wanted his independence. The business was to continue "under the style or firm of Nightingale Brothers," and in 1899 appears as such in print: "Nightingale Bros. builders, contractors, quarry masters."[11]

The business was beginning to have problems. A major setback, caused by the carelessness of one of the brothers, was the collapse of a crane into a quarry, resulting in the loss of both crane and quarry. A slowdown in demand did not help matters; and cash was tight. Whether these business

---

7. Thistlethwaite, pp. 70, 71.
8. *Barrett's Directory of Burnley, Nelson, Padiham, Colne and Barnoldswick*, 1893, p. 231.
9. *Barrett's Directory*, 1896, pp. 135, 136.
10. *The London Gazette*, April 9, 1897, p. 2036.
11. *Barrett's Directory*, 1899, p. 152.

factors or problems closer to home (a domineering father? a mistress?) caused Thomas to lose his patience and throw up his hands is unclear. But without any warning he disappeared.

Rumour had it that his secretary (or was it a seamstress?) went with him to America, where it is reasonable to suppose he would have contacted his Uncle John, who had immigrated to the United States in 1873. John Nightingale had established himself in Fall River, Massachusetts, where he became a successful cotton overseer at the Osborne Mills. A leading Freemason he was also a popular local politician, elected to both branches of the city government. This promising career was abruptly cut short. During a government meeting in 1903 in Boston he suffered a heart attack and died at his home.[12] Meanwhile, Thomas had written (1900?) from America to arrange for the financial upkeep of his Burnley family, putting their affairs in the hands of his younger brother, William, and promising to return when he had made some money. He never did. From time to time, he sent a five-dollar bill earmarked for one of the children, but that was about it.

Thomas's wife and now seven children – Edith aged 13, surviving twin Beth 9, Connie 7, Tom 3, the new twins Alice & Dora, 1, Kathleen 7 months – were thrown into confusion. His parents, brothers, and sisters were stunned. The abandonment of his wife and children threw a disapproving light on the whole family and, nonconformist "respectable" Victorians that they were, they felt it. Nevertheless, their first inclination was to rally round. With her now greatly reduced income Annie was obliged to move the family from their home at 163 Coal Clough Lane downhill to shabbier accommodations three blocks away.[13] What she did with Thomas's sixteen show dogs, amongst them Pomeranians and a Saint Bernard, is unknown. On a more positive note, within a few years she was able to move her household to a more suitable property at 42 St. Matthews Street[14] in the same neighborhood [Fig. 1.1]. It is unclear how she managed to afford this move; but her eldest daughter, Edith, may have helped. After working as an apprentice teacher in an elementary school and becoming a "Qualified Teacher," she had taken a position in a school for handicapped children.

12. *New York Times*, May 30, 1903.
13. Census, 1901.
14. *Barrett's Directory*, 1905, p. 198.

Annie Nightingale's refusal to allow her daughters to follow the usual custom of going to work "in the mill" and her insistence that, after a thorough schooling, they learn a trade or train to be teachers, are worth noting.

Although the family was well versed in Victorian respectability, business success, material rewards, and chapel activities, and some of them were in education as a route to self-improvement and social awareness, they could hardly be described as intellectual or highbrow. Beyond an interest in music making and concertgoing there is little evidence of concern for literature or the arts. It is hard to imagine that any of these hardworking, ostensibly strait-laced folks were familiar with the major literary figures of the time, though they may well have flinched at any mention of Oscar Wilde. Seriously committed attention to philosophy, literature, or arts and crafts did not appear in the family until Connie.

Early Days

At the same time as Annie Nightingale moved the family from the Beech Grove house, she removed Connie and her two elder sisters from Grant's School. William Milner Grant had opened this new fee-paying school, intended for the children of what might be termed the bourgeoisie of the town, in 1859 after poor health caused him to leave the headship of St. Peter's School. Edith went off to learn the tailoring trade, Beth stayed at home, and Connie transferred to the newly built free elementary school down Coal Clough Lane. Initiated and funded by the Town Council, and urged on by Connie's aunt's husband, Sharp Thornber, who chaired the Education Committee, construction had begun on this school, described as the "finest and best equipped in the Burnley District," by 1899.[15] It was from this brand-new school that Connie in 1904 won a municipal scholarship, a William Milner Grant's Scholars' Memorial Scholarship, to attend Burnley Grammar School,[16] taking with it a prize worth £5. She was Burnley's outstanding girl student.

---

15. *Barrett's Directory*, 1899, p. 18. The estimated cost was £14,000, the architect was W. A. Quarmby.
16. *Burnley Grammar School Annual Report*, 1906, p. 14.

Fig. 1.1. *42 St. Matthew Street, Burnley: Connie Nightingale's home during her school days. (Photo: Google Maps)*

At the grammar school Connie was in her element. A tireless student, she was remarkable for her powers of concentration, her enjoyment of languages, and delight in learning. The Burnley Grammar School Annual Report for 1906 reveals that in both 1905 and 1906 she won Stroyan Memorial Prizes for English Literature and in 1906 was clear top of Form IV A, ranked amongst the top four students in all eleven subjects[17] with the exception of Arithmetic, in which she placed seventh. An unprecedented mark of the excellence of her academic performance and leadership qualities was her appointment as "head boy" of the school in 1908, a promotion

---

17. Ibid., 1906, pp. 6, 14. She placed first in Latin, French, English, History, and Chemistry.

announced at the annual prize-giving in the unexpected and paradoxical phrase "the head boy is a girl."[18]

The following year she was awarded a scholarship designated for attendance at the University of Manchester, "a scholarship of the value of 35 pounds a year, tenable for three years at the University of Manchester"; this was one of a handful of awards "founded by Mrs. J. W. Phillips in memory of her late husband."[19] When it was discovered that the scholarship would not cover all the expenses of an academic year, she approached her uncle William – the uncle entrusted by her father with the financial welfare of the family – only to be brusquely told, "thee'd be better off wearing clogs and shawl and earning some brass: get weaving." This attitude enraged the grammar school's headmaster so much that he offered to make up the difference himself, an offer forestalled by Connie's successful uncle by marriage, Sharp Thornber, who stepped in.[20] That the decision to support Connie's enthusiasm for a university education was right-minded is underscored by her early success at the university.[21]

She had survived the dismay the children had felt when their father absconded to America, finding refuge and inspiration in her schoolwork. Encouraged by her Uncle Sharp, by her mother's determination, and by her sister Edith's example, as well as driven by her own diligence and thirst for knowledge, she had devoted herself consistently to her schoolwork and had reaped the rewards. She was now ready to sample life beyond the confines of a small industrial town: the opportunities of a well-established, highly regarded university and the riches of a dynamic commercial city lay open before her.

---

18. *Burnley Express*, December 12, 1908, p. 12.
19. *Burnley Grammar School Annual Report*, 1910, p. 13.
20. Thistlethwaite, p. 115.
21. *Burnley Grammar School Annual Report*, 1911, p. 14.

CHAPTER
2

MANCHESTER: THE OPENING WORLD

At the time of Connie's arrival in the city in 1909, Manchester was a thriving trading and manufacturing centre, not unlike Burnley in character but vastly larger and more ambitious. Many factors had been at play in the city's success: scientific and engineering knowledge, technical and mechanical innovation, craftsmanship, business know-how, municipal pride, philanthropic spirit, and a demanding work ethic, amongst others. Education and research had come to be highly valued. By the end of the eighteenth century Manchester Grammar School had introduced more scientific studies to the curriculum and James Watt had created the separate condenser engine, the instrument of a new power technology profitable for mining and manufacturing firms.

John Kennedy and James McConnell provide examples of the city's creative spirit. Textile machine builders and cotton spinners, they formed a business partnership which made the most of steam power, mechanical knowledge, and good business practice. In 1797 they set up the first of several prosperous factories and became the original Manchester cotton barons. Their leadership in science and business was echoed in their cultural activities. They joined the Manchester Mechanics Institute and the Manchester Literary and Philosophical Society. They became inspectors of the Manchester Infirmary and Lunatic Asylum. In religion they were Dissenters, and amongst Dissenters, Unitarians. These and other such networks enabled them to meet like-minded folks and offered opportunities for the exchange of ideas. Their ideas of leadership could be put to the test.

By the beginning of the nineteenth century the increased number of mills, factories, foundries, ironworks, and dwellings showed that Manchester was one of the front-runners in industry in England. There was no shortage of employment or of workers, and everywhere there were signs of prosperity. In 1851 the city sent no fewer than 191 exhibits to the Great Exhibition, a number exceeded only by Birmingham.[1] Politically the city was ruled by the Tories up to midcentury, but by the 1870s power had passed to a coalition of Liberals amongst whom Unitarians were prominent. Amongst other liberal proposals the emancipation of women was coming to the fore. Emily Pankhurst (1858–1928), born in Moss Side, a densely populated and notorious district near the city centre, attended her first suffrage meeting in 1872, setting out on her path to the leadership of the suffragette movement. She founded the Women's Franchise League in 1889 and in 1903 the Women's Social and Political Union, activities which would not have been without interest to the young Connie Nightingale.

The city's active industrial and political life was matched by advances in architecture and the arts. By 1856 the palazzo-style Free Trade Hall, built to commemorate the work of Lancashire mill owner Richard Cobden's Anti-Corn Law League and the 1846 abolition of the Corn Laws, had opened. Public buildings became expansive statements of wealth, personal or corporate, and civic pride. A majestic town hall decorated on the exterior with statues of historical figures and provided inside with a council chamber, administrative offices, and an apartment for the Lord Mayor, was built in striking neo-Gothic style (1868–77). It was matched by the John Rylands Library, another neo-Gothic pile, on nearby Deansgate. Rapidly built (1899–1900) by Enriqueta Rylands in memory of her husband, the library is famous for its collection of mediaeval illuminated manuscripts and papyri. Closer yet to the town hall was the imposing Midland Hotel, built (1898–1903) by the Midland Railway Company. The Edwardian baroque style of this architecture, as lavishly ornate as that of the John Rylands Library, was a suitable backdrop for the partnership formed here in 1904 be-

---

1. Margaret C. Jacob, *The First Knowledge Economy: Human Capital and the European Economy, 1750–1850* (Cambridge: Cambridge University Press, 2014), 114 n. 11.

tween Charles Rolls and Henry Royce as they launched their famous car company.

News of the city's growth and activities was reported by the *Manchester Guardian,* one of the more intelligent and articulate national newspapers. Reports appeared on the political, economic, and social news of the day alongside commentary on the city's architectural landscape, on museums, art, plays, and other entertainments. Highly regarded was the extensive reporting of concerts given at the Free Trade Hall by the Hallé orchestra. Brainchild of Sir Charles Hallé (conductor 1858–95) the orchestra acquired such a glittering reputation that in 1899 it was able to lure the great Hans Richter (conductor 1899–1911) away from the Vienna Philharmonic. It is fair to say that by 1900 Manchester was firmly established as the cultural as well as the industrial leader of the North of England. Such was the creative and industrious city where the seventeen-year-old Connie Nightingale came to live in 1909.

The University

The University of Manchester too was coming into its own. It had begun life in midcentury as a technical college, Owens College, named after John Owens, cotton merchant and wealthy benefactor. Granted a new charter in 1903 it became the Victoria University of Manchester. Strong in the humanities as well as the sciences and textile studies, its Professor of Greek in 1909 was Ronald Burrows, recently (1908) arrived from the Chair of Greek at University College, Cardiff. Amongst the new intake of classical scholars was the precocious Connie Nightingale: the first and only girl to have been head boy of Burnley Grammar School.

Ashburne Hall

Connie took up residence in one of the university's recently established residential halls for women, Ashburne Hall. Founded in 1900 as a residence for women students by Manchester worthies, amongst them C. P. Scott, famous editor of the *Manchester Guardian* (now *The Guardian*), Ashburne Hall occupied an imposing nineteenth-century building (classical façade with Ionic porch) built for a businessman of means [Fig. 2.1]. Subsequent new structures have greatly enhanced the hall and its campus. Here, Connie met a group of like-minded, intelligent, and hardworking young women committed, as she was, to women's education. Set up on the same organisational pattern as the halls for men, Ashburne had been opened in 1900 by Eleanor Sidgwick, Principal of Newnham College, Cambridge. A new wing dedicated in 1910 by Emily Penrose, Principal of Somerville College, Oxford, effectively provided Ashburnians with links to the two great English universities. At the time of Connie's arrival, the Warden of Ashburne Hall was the charismatic Phoebe Sheavyn.

Phoebe Sheavyn (1865–1968)

Born in Atherstone, a town on the Warwickshire–Leicestershire border, Sheavyn was raised in modest circumstances (her father was a draper) not unlike Connie Nightingale's in Burnley.[2] Determined to avoid the life of a live-in assistant in another draper's shop (one of the few opportunities available to young women of her social status in Victorian England), she struggled to equip herself as a teacher. After a brief appointment in a primary school in Leicester, she taught part-time at a boarding school in Stroud before finding a job as governess to the children of the architect Thomas Edward Collcutt. Encouraged by him and his wife, she studied at London's Birkbeck College in the evenings and after two years passed the London Matriculation exams.

The way to a university degree then opened unexpectedly when the University College of Wales at Aberystwyth announced a competition for scholarships for women. Again encouraged by the Collcutts, Sheavyn took the exams, won a scholarship, and entered the university in 1887. With her B.A. in hand (1889), and a ringing endorsement from Professor C. H.

2, Brian Sheavyn, "Dr Phoebe Sheavyn – Her History" (2007), bound manuscript, archival material, National Library of Wales, Aberystwyth, Ceredigion, NLW ex 2599; Enid Huws Jones, "Sheavyn Phoebe Ann Beale (1865–1968)," *Oxford Dictionary of National Biography* (Oxford: Oxford University Press, 2004), online edition (2009).

Fig. 2.1. *Ashburne Hall, University of Manchester, where Connie Nightingale lived as an undergraduate. (Photo: Google Maps)*

Herford, Professor of English Language and Literature, Sheavyn was well launched:

> Both in grasp of facts, in critical capacity, in literary force and refinement, and in general power of mind, I consider her without question the most remarkable student, of either sex, with whom I have ever in my department had to do.   – 18th December 1889.

After teaching for a year in a "proprietary" school[3] in Gravesend, and a further two outside London at Haberdashers' Aske's School for Girls, she returned to Aberystwyth and left again in 1894 with an M.A. in English and French. Placed top of the list at Aberystwyth, she took an adventurous tack when she won a scholarship, followed by a fellowship, to Bryn Mawr College near Philadelphia in Pennsylvania. She taught and studied

---

3. Proprietary schools were private, fee-paying, for-profit institutions offering vocational education, sometimes church-related.

at Bryn Mawr for two years. Returning from America in 1896 she found employment in Oxford, again thanks to Professor Herford, working on the *English Dialect Dictionary* with Professor Joseph Wright. A year later she was appointed the first resident tutor in English at Somerville College.

Her ten years in Oxford were both happy and frustrating: happy in that she enjoyed the daily contact with intellectually stimulating young colleagues, frustrating in that she found the university's attitude to women condescending. Compared with Aberystwyth, where she had seen coeducation prosper, and with Bryn Mawr, where women's education was accorded full recognition, Oxford seemed behind the times. Yet these years were also productive. Taking a sabbatical year (1905–6) she completed work for her London D.Litt. with a thesis on the "Economic Position of the Professional Writer under Elizabeth," a thesis which, revised and expanded, was published by Manchester University Press.[4] The book gained, and retained, a reputation as a meticulously written early contextual literary study. Sheavyn left Oxford in 1907 to take up a new appointment at Manchester as university lecturer, tutor to women students, and Warden of Ashburne Hall [Fig. 2.2] – an appointment doubtless recommended by the Principal of Somerville College, Emily Penrose, and supported, once more, by her Aberystwyth professor, Professor C. H. Herford, who had left Aberystwyth for Manchester in 1901. Sheavyn was forty-two years old. No appointment could have been more suited to her talents and temperament. By the example of her own life, she set the pace for the young women in her charge.

The Ashburne women, some fifty in number in 1909, thoroughly appreciated Sheavyn's intellectual strengths, her determined belief in women's education and women's rights, and her concern for their welfare as individuals. She saw them daily; she held discussion and reading groups; she led morning prayers; she brought distinguished visitors to speak and converse with them. For their part, the women demonstrated their ability to compete with men by working all out, engaging in every activity open to them. Studies came first, but close behind were extracurricular activities:

---

4. Phoebe Sheavyn, *The Literary Profession in the Elizabethan Age* (Manchester: Manchester University Press, 1909; 2nd ed. revd. J. W. Saunders, 1967).

Fig. 2.2. *Phoebe Sheavyn, Warden of Ashburne Hall and Connie Nightingale's mentor.*
(Photo: Courtesy Ashburne Hall, Manchester University archives)

debating societies, political discussions (with the Manchester suffragette marches an obvious point of reference), bike rides, other physical exertions, and service to the community. Not a moment was to be lost. Connie threw herself headlong into this maelstrom of activity: she became a member of the House Committee; she organised the first cricket team (with the help of men from Dalton Hall, the university residence hall for Quaker men) and captained the side; she helped with the professors' children's parties, and with the work of the University Settlement in Ancoats, one of the poorer districts in the city, in which her Greek professor, Professor Burrows, was deeply involved.[5] In the fervid atmosphere of Ashburne Hall, Connie would have been fully aware of contemporary events: the suffrage demonstrations, the women's movement, the railway strikes, the international political crises.

Illness and Revival: The Gimsons

The stimulating environment in which these seriously committed young women led their hectic lives inevitably led to overwork and lack of sleep. Some Ashburne women burnt the candle at both ends so frequently that their health suffered, and they were sent home for a rest. At some point during her third year Connie suffered a breakdown which threatened her eyesight (she was unable to read); this was severe enough for the Faculty of Arts to grant her deferral of her final examinations from 1912 to 1913. Since the family situation in Burnley was not thought likely to assist her recovery, she went to live for a good part of academic 1911–12 with a wealthy couple, Sydney and Jeannie Gimson, in their large house in Leicester and at their summer place, Stoneywell Cottage, in the country. It is uncertain who introduced Connie to the Gimsons, but of Connie's two acquaintances in Manchester most likely to have moved in the same circles as the Gimsons, Phoebe Sheavyn and Ronald Burrows, Phoebe Sheavyn is the more likely to have been responsible.

Sydney Gimson (1860–1938) was the third son of Josiah (1818–83) and Sarah Gimson. In 1842 Josiah and his brother Benjamin had founded Gimson and Company, manufacturers of heavy machinery. Soon renamed the Vulcan Works, it became the largest employer in Leicester, well known for its sympathetic treatment of its workers. Josiah was a member of the local committee supporting women's suffrage, a freethinker, a socialist, and a secularist. One of the leaders of the Leicester Secular Society, whose tenets emphasised belief in an "inclusive and plural society free from religious

---

5. The settlement movement was a social and reformist enterprise aiming to bring together the poor and university graduates through educational programmes promoting social mobility. Settlement communities sprang up first in London in 1885, followed by Edinburgh and Glasgow in 1889 and Manchester in 1895.

privilege, prejudice and discrimination,"[6] he was the prime mover in, and major contributor to, the construction of the Leicester Secular Hall (1881).

Sydney followed his father into the business, and he too was a radical. In his long (1883–1938) tenure of the presidency of the Secular Society he regularly spoke up for the society's beliefs: freedom of religion, freedom of speech, freedom from prejudice, equality of the sexes, equality of opportunity, a bedrock personal morality. More of an individualist than a socialist, he favoured municipal responsibility and argued for the creation of parks, museums, sanitation systems, and the like. He brought leading intellectual figures to Leicester to address the society, William Morris amongst them. Morris's talk on Art and Socialism at the Secular Hall in 1884 made a deep impression on many, including Sydney's younger brother Ernest.

A student at the Leicester School of Art and an apprentice architect, Ernest Gimson (1864–1919) shared Morris's views on socialism, moved to London, and became a respected figure in the Art and Crafts movement. Between 1897 and 1899 he built Stoneywell Cottage, now (2021) a National Trust site, for Sydney and his wife, Jeannie, in the Arts and Crafts style. In all likelihood it was here in the tranquillity of the countryside that Connie Nightingale was able to rest and recuperate.

In Leicester she was exposed to, and doubtless relished, the activities of the Secular Society, where she met many adherents and sympathisers – artists, writers, suffragettes, and statesmen.[7] Her intellectual and social horizons had already been expanded by her university experiences, but in the company of the Gimsons they were broadened unimaginably. Connie and they became great friends. Recovered from her breakdown, with eyesight restored, Connie returned to Manchester for her final year, graduating with a B.A. in 1913. Compensating for lost time she continued for a further year and received an M.A. in Classics in 1914.

Determined to pursue a career in education, she found employment – shortly before the outbreak of World War I – on the teaching staff of Lady Manners School in Bakewell, Derbyshire, one of the first schools in England to practice coeducation. During the war, as teaching staff throughout

---

6. Leicester Secular Society, http://leicestersecularsociety.org.uk/, accessed August 14, 2021.
7. *Burnley Express*, December 22, 1967.

the country left their schools to join the armed forces, she moved to take up a more senior appointment as the Classics teacher at Bootham School, a Quaker school in York. At the end of the war her commitment to the Quaker way of life, her interest in the cause of peace, and her sympathy for the plight of refugees led her to seek a role for herself at the Paris Peace Conference beginning in January 1919. Nothing was to hold her back.

CHAPTER
3

BEYOND BRITAIN: PARIS AND CONSTANTINOPLE

At some point Connie became a Quaker, perhaps as an undergraduate in contact with the Quaker men in Dalton Hall, or more probably when she was teaching in York. The Quaker archives in Manchester and York reveal little. In York, in addition to the well-known Quaker boarding schools, Bootham for boys and The Mount for girls, there was a wide circle of socially and politically influential Quakers with whom Connie later came to feel at home. Wherever and whenever it was that she became a Quaker, it soon became clear that she was committed to Quaker views on peace, freedom, compassion, individual honesty, and integrity. We may well believe it was these values that led her to the 1919 Peace Conference in Paris, and after that to her work in Constantinople in 1919–20.

Paris

The Paris Peace Conference opened in January 1919 and lasted formally till January of the following year. US President Woodrow Wilson, however, as well as other leading figures left immediately after the signing of the treaty involving Germany, the Treaty of Versailles, on June 28.[1] Connie Nightingale attended the conference as an assistant to the delegation of

1. Margaret Macmillan, *Paris 1919: Six Months that Changed the World* (New York: Random House, 2003), *passim*; for Greece's interest and involvement see Nikolaos Petsalis-Diomidis, *Greece at the Paris Peace Conference* (1919) (Thessaloniki: Institute for Balkan Studies, 1978).

Fig. 3.1. *Ronald Burrows, Connie Nightingale's Professor of Greek at Manchester University. (Photo: Glasgow,* Ronald Burrows, *frontispiece)*

the Ecumenical Patriarchate of Constantinople and the National Council of Unredeemed Greeks (that is, ethnic Greeks living under repressive Ottoman rule, and thus termed "Unredeemed"). This delegation argued the case for those who had lived in Thrace and Asia Minor prior to the war and had been driven from their homes by the Turks; in 1912 these had numbered 2.5 million.[2] We do not know precisely what her duties were, but according to family sources she acted as an interpreter[3] and administrative assistant.

2. London Committee of Unredeemed Greeks [G. Marchetti and others], *The Liberation of the Greek People in Turkey* (Manchester and London: Norbury, Natzio & Co., 1919), p. 11; [B. Musuris Ghikis and others], *The Unredeemed Greeks before the Peace Conference: Memoranda of the Œcumenical Patriarchate and the National Council of Unredeemed Greeks* (Paris: G. Dussardier & P. Frank, 1919).

3. Frank Thistlethwaite, *A Lancashire Family Inheritance* (Cambridge: F. Thistlethwaite, 1996), p. 118.

Fig. 3.2. *Ronald Burrows at his holiday cottage in North Wales. (Photo: Glasgow,* Ronald Burrows*)*

How did she become involved in this? Relevant archives have not yet produced direct evidence, but a series of connectible facts suggest an answer. Like most of her contemporaries she had been deeply affected by the war. She was moved to action especially by the plight of refugees, and amongst refugees by the Greek refugees from Turkey. Wondering what to do and how to help, it is reasonable to think she would turn for advice to Ronald Burrows, her Professor of Greek at Manchester [Figs. 3.1, 3.2]. She knew Burrows primarily as a scholar and as her academic mentor. But she had also worked alongside him in the University Settlement in efforts to bring young people who lived in the slums together with university students. Her instincts for social reform were like his. Moreover, with reference to problems in Greece, she knew that Burrows was well connected with highly placed Greek politicians.

Burrows had been appointed Principal of King's College London in 1913. He was well known as a friend of Greece through his scholarship, his archaeological work in Greece, his fluency in both Classical and Modern

Greek, and his frequent articles in the British press supporting liberal policies in Greece.[4] What's more he was known to be a friend of Eleftherios Venizelos, for long periods (1910–15, 1917–20, 1924, 1928–32, 1933) the Prime Minister of Greece, with whom he exchanged cables almost daily during World War I.[5] In fact, Venizelos was so impressed by Burrows's intellect, knowledge, and support of his (Venizelos's) political views that in 1916, while out of office and exiled from Athens, he invited Burrows to be the representative in London of the revolutionary Greek government in Salonika.[6] Since Connie was looking for ways to help refugee Greeks, and since she knew that Venizelos, a friend of her old Manchester professor, would be leading the Greek delegation at the Paris Conference, it is likely she would have consulted Burrows.

Burrows possibly mentioned her to Venizelos himself, or more certainly to another influential Greek and friend of Venizelos, Konstantinos Spanoudis. Spanoudis lived in London part of the year, was frequently in touch with Burrows. and was a member of the London Committee of Unredeemed Greeks.[7] He was also President of the Central Committee of Unredeemed Greeks during the Paris negotiations.[8] The good offices of either Spanoudis or Venizelos offer potential explanations of how Connie came to be present at the Paris talks. Given that Spanoudis sponsored her in Constantinople after the conference and given the friendship that developed between her and his family, Spanoudis is the more probable of the two.

Constantinople and the Spanoudis

Born in Constantinople in 1871, Konstantinos Spanoudis studied political science in France and Italy before returning to Constantinople to launch one of the most important Greek newspapers in the city, *Proodos* (Progress),

---

4. At Kings College Burrows established a new chair of Modern Greek, as well as others in Slavonic Studies, Portuguese, and Spanish; George Glasgow, *Ronald Burrows: A Memoir* (London: Nisbet & Co., 1924), pp. 212–13.
5. Ibid., p. 237.
6. Ibid., pp. 242 ff.
7. London Committee, p. 11. Another member of the London Committee was the wealthy Helena Schilizzi, who married Venizelos in 1921.
8. [Ghikis and others], p. 19.

in 1904.⁹ When in 1921 monarchists in Greece wanted Spanoudis tried for treason, his supporters in Constantinople objected: "opponents of King Constantine amongst the Greek population of Constantinople [were] aroused by the arrest of M. Spanoudis, editor of the Greek newspaper *Proodos*, and vice-President of the League of National Defense."¹⁰ In Paris Connie evidently came to know him well. Following her work at the conference, she went to Constantinople to work on *Proodos*, reporting on the influx and resettlement of Christian refugees, most of whom were Greeks.¹¹ In Constantinople she became a good friend of the family, a friendship that continued when – after the 1919–22 Greco-Turkish war and the confiscation of *Proodos* by the Turks – the Konstantinos Spanoudis branch of the family left Constantinople. They settled in Athens, where in 1924 Spanoudis joined with other Constantinopolitans to set up a sports club named AEK (the K standing for Constantinople) of which he became the first President. AEK has become one of the most famous sports clubs in Greece.

Judging from Connie's description of the Spanoudis family in correspondence with David Russell, they were brilliant, enterprising, and eccentric. The father was a successful newspaper- and businessman, the mother, Mme. Sophia Spanoudi (1878–1952), a distinguished music critic (herself an accomplished pianist), was considered the cleverest woman of letters in Greece. An eccentric, she took little care of her everyday appearance, often looking "like a charwoman" but on social occasions quite the opposite. A daughter, Ninitza, equally brilliant, and fluent in English, devoted her energies to sports and wrote a book on the subject – *Athleticism: The New Religion*. Though a great fan of boxing, her long fingernails were "a

---

9. The circulation of *Proodos* in 1920 was 2,500–3,000, in line with the three other Greek newspapers in Constantinople: see *Editor & Publisher*, January 8, 1920.
10. *The Fourth Estate* (weekly newspaper), July 2, 1921,
11. Noted by K. Olwen Rees in his tribute at the memorial service for Miss Nightingale at The Friends Meeting House, Euston Road, London, February 29, 1968. Some 150 people, several of whom spoke movingly about her, attended the service, details of which were printed together with the programme of an earlier memorial service held at Dr. Williams' School, Dolgellau, Merioneth, on January 31, 1968. Amongst the refugees there were also numerous Armenians and Russians. Connie's work for the Friends War Victims Relief efforts offers another example of the Quaker commitment to peace.

clear indication that she never plays games herself."[12] An uncle of Ninitza's, Alexander Spanoudis, was one of the best-known doctors in the Near East, a great Anglophile, English speaker, and avid reader of English literature. Connie spent many weeks with him and his wife at their summer home on one of the Princes Islands, Antigoni (modern Burgazada), in the Sea of Marmara. For the efficiency and punctuality of the ferry systems to the islands Connie was full of praise.

Few details of Connie's life in Constantinople have come to light. In the same letter to David Russell, she mentioned "the two summers I spent there 1919–1920"; so it seems she was based in Constantinople for a little over a year, presumably from June 1919 (when many participants left Paris after the Treaty of Versailles was signed) until September 1920. She lived in the heart of the city, close to the British Embassy, near the Pera Palas Otel, which she recommended to Russell.[13] In answer to Russell's enquiries about health and specifically about inoculations she remarked:

> I never had any inoculations even in the years 1919–1920 and did not suffer in any way. At that time there was every chance of illness because not only was the war not finished but the allied forces were there, and the Russian refugees were flocking in during part of the time. My sister who was with me had never been vaccinated and she had no touch of anything. Personally, I would not have them. The water is so very good. Abdul Hamid was so terrified of germs that he conferred a great benefit upon the city by helping good waters to be tapped.[14]

A direct, if fleeting, glimpse of refugee work is provided by Alice, Connie's younger sister, who in her memoir writes of the five months in 1924 she spent in Greece helping with refugee work.[15] Alice lived with a doctor, his wife, and four children – an introduction provided by Connie's Greek connections – and travelled around the countryside with the father and

---

12. University of St. Andrews Library, David Russell Collection (hereafter SAUL), ECN to DR, March 23, 1932, ms38515/5/96/2.
13. SAUL, ECN to DR, April 30, 1935, ms38515/5/96/3.
14. Sultan Abdulhamid II (1876–1909) had repaired the city's fountains, cisterns, and water conduits. Constantinople was ahead of most of Europe in recognising the hygienic value of fresh water.
15. Alice Nightingale, *Mother 1861–1945* (printed privately, December 1980), pp. 40–1.

another doctor on the lookout for wandering refugees. On several occasions they found refugees hiding under hedges and, once, a woman giving birth to a boy. Most of Alice's time was spent on keeping up the registration of refugees. "Handicapped by not speaking Greek – I only had a very small vocabulary but I could write in Greek so was put on to keeping a register."

Connie's tasks at the Paris Peace Conference had included participating in discussions and acting as an interpreter when her knowledge of Modern Greek, doubtless learnt from Professor Burrows, came into play. In Constantinople her Modern Greek, although different from the Asiatic dialects of many of the refugees, would have been invaluable. Refugee work required helpers to register fugitives, find and distribute clothing, food, and medicine, and provide schooling and adult education. Housing especially was in short supply, with every available space allocated to refugees and brought into use: hotels, churches, other places of worship, monasteries, breweries, barracks, railway stations, factories, prisons. For local communities where refugees were billeted, programmes explaining the newcomers' histories and cultures became imperative. These are the problems with which Connie was concerned until her return to England in September 1920. There she immediately took up a new teaching appointment at The Mount School in York.[16]

No sooner had she settled in than she was asked, and given leave early in 1921, to assist a delegation led by Patriarch Dorotheos of Constantinople in London. Following the repudiation of the Treaty of Sèvres (August 10, 1920) by the Turkish nationalists led by Mustafa Kemal Atatürk, this delegation had come to England to take part in negotiations regarding a new treaty. The conference was cut short, however, by the sudden death of Patriarch Dorotheos on March 6,[17] and no new treaty was agreed with the Turkish Republic until the Treaty of Lausanne two years later.

16. Borthwick Institute, York, Mount School Archive (hereafter BIY), Minute Book 1910–27, MOU 1/2/1/5, Minutes of Meeting of General Committee 21/5/1920 registering Connie's acceptance of appointment.
17. Dimitris Stamatopoulos, trans. Nakas Iannis, "Greek Orthodox Patriarchate of Constantinople, 1839–1923," in *Encyclopedia of the Hellenic World*, vol. 3, *Constantinople* (Athens: Foundation of the Hellenic World, 2008), online at http://constantinople.ehw.gr/Forms/fLemmaBody.aspx?lemmaid=11472, accessed July 15, 2021.

Connie's contributions to this London conference cannot have lasted more than a couple of months. However, it has been reported that in recognition of her work for the organisations representing the Unredeemed Greeks, she received an extraordinary mark of recognition: she was awarded the Gold Cross of the Holy Sepulchre by the Patriarch of Jerusalem, an award rarely given to anyone not Greek by birth.[18]

---

18 See, e.g., *Burnley Express,* 29 December 1962, p. 9.

CHAPTER
4

ALEXIS ALADIN

Returning from Constantinople in late September 1920 with her sister Kathleen – for whom she had also arranged a job tutoring the children of a Greek doctor – Connie met a Russian officer who was to have a profound effect on her life. His name was Alexis Feodorovich Aladin. They fell into conversation after their train, the Orient Express, was halted at Trieste by trouble on the line (a bridge over the River Po was down), and all passengers were transferred to a steamer to take them to Venice to resume their journey.

An important political figure in prerevolutionary Russia, Aladin (1873–1927) was born into an agricultural family, his father a landowning farmer who had fallen on hard times, his mother a devout Orthodox Christian who reconciled her Christian faith with a fervent belief in mysticism, folklore, magic, and myth.[1]

Aladin had been heavily influenced at school by the work of Nikolai Chernyshevsky, whose writings (including the 1863 novel *What Is to Be*

---

1. The story of Aladin's life from boyhood in Simbirsk and undergraduate days at the University of Kazan, through antigovernment activities, exile in Europe, leadership of the Peasant Party (the Trudoviks) in the 1st Duma (April–July 1906), exile again, efforts as businessman and journalist in England, and the slow decline in his later years is well described by Reginald Frank Christian in his book *Alexis Aladin: The Tragedy of Exile* (Ottawa: Legas, 1999), hereafter Christian. More details of Aladin's life can be found in earlier articles by R. F. Christian: "Alexis Aladin, Trudovik Leader in the First Duma: Materials for a Biography (1873–1920)," *Oxford Slavonic Papers* 21 (1988): 131–52; and "Alexis Aladin: The Last Years (1920–1927)," *Oxford Slavonic Papers* 23 (1990): 79–97.

Done – a title reused by Lenin in 1902 for his own political pamphlet) led him to join groups antagonistic to the government and to participate in rebellious activities for which he paid the price. Expelled from school, he was nevertheless able to enter Kazan University, where after distinguishing himself in his studies (Chemistry, Mathematics, and Physics) he again got himself into hot water and had to leave. Now identified as a subversive, he was watched by the police, and it was not long before he was arrested and put on trial (1895). On completing a nine-month prison sentence he returned to his hometown of Simbirsk (renamed Ulyanovsk in 1924), a provincial capital on the Volga. Though a city which had declined over the years, it is worth noting that Alexander Kerensky, the leader of the 1917 Provisional Government, was born in Simbirsk in 1881, and that Lenin himself was one of Aladin's schoolboy contemporaries. When shortly after his return home Aladin discovered he had been sentenced to three years internal exile, he left the country.

He fled first to France, where he made a disreputable living from the manufacture and sale of fake antiques. After a while he moved to Belgium to work in an engineering factory where his tasks ranged from work on the shop floor to writing scientific articles. Dissatisfied at the lack of any way forward for his political ambitions he moved in 1900 to London. His knowledge of English was limited, but he learnt quickly, read widely in the Reading Room at the British Museum – where he surely met Lenin during his stay in London (1902–3) – and began to earn a living teaching Russian, translating Russian documents, and writing. He came in touch with many other Russian exiles, who commented on his zeal for reform and for compromise. Gaining in confidence and authority he presided in early 1905 at a meeting of the London branch of the Russian Social Democratic Labour Party, speaking in severe terms about the czarist regime. Meanwhile, the political situation in Russia went from bad to worse with military defeats in the Far East, mutiny in the fleet, and strikes here and there culminating in a general strike that paralysed Saint Petersburg. The czar's reply to these disruptions was to offer a constitution and an expanded electorate empowered to choose an Assembly (a Duma).

Encouraged by a political amnesty Aladin returned to Russia in late 1905 and in Simbirsk was invited to represent the local electorate in the

Fig. 4.1. *A raffish Alexis Feodorovich Aladin (note cigarette and suede gloves) in Saint Petersburg, 1906. (Photo: Courtesy John Rylands University of Manchester Library, Special Collections)*

Duma. He also met and fell in love with Elizaveta (Liza) Ananieva. She, just a year younger than he, and the daughter of a wealthy Simbirsk businessman, was already married and the mother of two children. Though brought up in a bourgeois atmosphere where money and class counted for everything, she held more liberal views than most of her family. When the First Duma opened in April, Aladin, recognised already as a savvy political organiser and spellbinding orator,[2] became the leader of the Peasant Party, the Trudoviks [Fig. 4.1]. This party, echoing Aladin's views, stood for agrarian reforms aimed at replacing the feudal system with a capitalistic system based on individual ownership of the land. The Duma, however,

---

2. For which Sergei Konovalov (1899–1982), Professor of Russian at Oxford University (1945–68), vouched in no uncertain terms.

was short-lived, its political proposals too liberal for the czar, who dissolved it in early July. At the time Aladin was in London serving as one of a handful of Duma delegates at an Interparliamentary Conference important enough to be held in the Palace of Westminster and addressed by the British Prime Minister. On the dissolution of the Duma other leaders – those in Saint Petersburg – fled to Finland. Aladin tried to join them in a return to Russia but, noting the presence of Russian agents in Helsinki and unwilling to risk more imprisonment (or assassination), returned to London. By the late summer of 1906 Liza, unhappy in her marriage, was looking to divorce her husband, and joined Aladin. But when he left early the following year for a lecture tour in America she returned to Russia and her children. In November they were together again in Belgium (he on another lecture tour), and December saw them back in London. Penniless, and with little prospect of work for him, they were rescued by funds from Liza's family in Simbirsk. They married on January 27, 1908, in the Uspensky Church of the Russian Embassy.

For the next few years Aladin stitched together a precarious living as journalist, lecturer, manager of a business marketing a new milk product resembling yoghurt, importer of caviar and other Russian fish products, partner in an engineering firm building motorboats (Moonbeams Ltd., 1911–14), and other schemes. Willing to try his hand at almost any enterprise, he seems to have been unable to sustain any particular interest. At the outbreak of war in 1914 his requests to the Russian ambassador to be allowed to return to Russia were rejected. When he turned again to the lecture circuit, large audiences up and down Britain attended his talks, a major theme of which was "Russia and the War," in which he repeatedly emphasised the need for friendship between Britain and Russia and each's recognition of the other's contributions to the war effort.

His ongoing conversations with British and Russian officials resulted in an invitation from the British government to accompany a party of Russian authors and journalists visiting Britain in early 1916.[3] The Russian party included Vladimir Nabokov (father of the Russian American poet and novelist of the same name), who had been a colleague of Aladin's in the First

---

3. John Rylands Library (hereafter JRL), Box 32, AA to ECN, October 25, 1923.

Fig. 4.2. *Alexis Aladin (at right) with Vladimir Dmitrievich Nabokov in 1906, members of the First Russian Duma.*
(Photo: Romanov Empire Historical Society, www.romanovempire.org)

Duma [Fig. 4.2], and M. E. Yegorov, foreign editor of *Novoye Vremya* (*New Times*), a literary and political newspaper published in Saint Petersburg. Aladin travelled with the party around Britain and France and impressed Yegorov enough to be asked to write articles about the British and the French war effort for the Russian paper. As a result, Aladin became a regular contributor to *Novoye Vremya*, and some thirty articles by him appeared during 1916 and 1917 [Fig. 4.3]. The paper was abruptly closed by Lenin in October 1917.

On various occasions in the first six months of 1917 Aladin inquired at the Foreign Office and the War Office about the possibility of his visiting the Western Front as a war correspondent, requests which were granted. In similar vein, he pressed to be allowed to go back to Russia. In the increasingly tense situation in Saint Petersburg, marked by sharp differences between antiwar left-wing groups and Kerensky's Provisional Government, the British ambassador, Sir George Buchanan, suggested that more moderate Russian voices such as Aladin's might be helpful. With this diplomatic support Aladin returned to Russia under British auspices and in a British army lieutenant's uniform – without, however, badges of rank or other insignia – in July 1917. It is unclear what his instructions were, but presumably the British government hoped he could mediate between Kerensky and the leftists and in so doing discern the shape of the plans and motives of each of the groups. But his early (August) involvement with General Lavr Kornilov, Commander of the Army of the Provisional Government,[4] in a suspected rightist coup against that government, did him no favours either with his old leftist political friends or with Kerensky.

He had enjoyed the prospect of government service in a putative Council for National Defence chaired by Kerensky;[5] and as Minister for Foreign Affairs in a reconstructed Provisional Government of reconciliation[6] under Kerensky's leadership. His high hopes of an important political future were apparently well founded. When identified, however, as a member of Kornilov's entourage, he was arrested. Released in late November (after the Bolshevik coup d'état) along with other detainees including Kornilov, he made his way south to the Cossack town of Novocherkassk, some twenty miles from Rostov. From here reassembled anti-Bolshevik elements launched a military offensive with a hastily gathered volunteer army, comprised mainly of remnants of the czar's army.

Throughout 1918 and 1919 the war raged back and forth amidst ferocious fighting (no prisoners), towns changing hands again and again. Kornilov was killed and replaced by General Anton Denikin. Other anti-Bolshevik generals gathered troops: General Popov an army of Cossacks, and General Denisov the so-called Don Army of the South. Aladin volunteered for action, participated in the fighting, was decorated for bravery,

---

4. Kornilov seems to have enjoyed Aladin's company: George [Georgij Mihajlovič] Katkov, *Russia 1917, the Kornilov Affair: Kerensky and the Break-up of the Russian Army* (London: Longman, 1980), 62.
5. Ibid., 180.
6. Sir George Buchanan, *My Mission to Russia*, 2 vols. (London and New York: Cassell & Co., 1923), 183.

Fig. 4.3. *Alexis Aladin in social attire, 1916. (Photo: Courtesy University of St. Andrews Library Special Collections, ms38515/7/5/7/7)*

and was awarded the title of "honorary Cossack." Despite the arrival during 1919 of a British Military Mission and the provision of tanks, equipment, and medical supplies to the White Army (the volunteers), by early 1920 the Whites were in retreat. In April General Denikin resigned and was replaced by General Pyotr Wrangel, a former member of the Imperial Guard, who did his best to steady the shattered anti-Bolshevik armies. As the White Armies collapse gathered pace, Aladin, now dignified with the title Head of the Sevastopol Political Section of the Political Unit of the Staff of the Commander-in-Chief of the Don Army of South Russia, retreated with them to the Crimea and had a hand in organising the resistance and subsequent evacuation of the remains of the Army of the South.

At the time, then, that this widely travelled, widely read, politically active, multilingual, anglophile Russian soldier met Connie Nightingale he was on his way to Paris as General Wrangel's emissary [Fig. 4.4]. He and Connie fell into conversation and found much in common – literature, poetry, politics, internationalism, nature, mysticism. To judge by the volume of the correspondence which ensued there was a sense of kinship between them from the start. Details of their meeting are best described in Connie's own words:

> My sister Kathleen (7 years younger than I am) and I left Constantinople Sept 20th 1920 on the Orient Express. At that time eleven visas were necessary for anyone travelling Constantinople to Calais. News came through that the bridge over the Po, owing to floods in N. Italy, had been rendered useless and later at night we were asked to get out of the trains at Trieste and walk to a Lloyd Triesteno boat coming from Malay which would take us to Venice. It was a glorious moonlight night. As Kathleen and I were standing on deck a white-haired gentleman came up to us and told us that there was a strike on board and no cabins were going to be opened that night and we should not sail until 6 a.m. the next day. He asked if he might show us the way down to the saloons where passengers were already settling down for the night. As we entered the saloon, absolutely packed, someone in khaki uniform got up from his seat and offered it to me. At first I demurred but he said "you had better take it now or somebody else will. I am an old campaigner and can sleep anywhere." He squatted on the floor and I offered him a coat I was carrying for a pillow, remarking it was the least I could do for a British soldier whereupon he declared he was not British. Without thinking I said "Are you Russian?" and he nodded Yes. In the morning when we awoke most folks had gone out of the saloon but our faithful white-haired Mr. Yeomans who was travelling from Malay and had six daughters there, came along to guide us this time to breakfast. Later on deck the Russian, Mr. Aladin, and Mr. Yeomans chatted with us until Mr. Y. had to go to look after his luggage – quantities – but not before he had advised us of a very nice hotel in Venice suitable for 2 (to him) young girls unaccompanied. We said goodbye and Aladin took us to the hotel. We had a meal and then Aladin offered to go down to the station and book our tickets for Paris. He came back and we all walked into St. Mark's square for coffee and soon, by chance, Mr. Yeomans came along. He had found accommodation in some hotel but no meals had been ready so he had come out in search. We said goodbye about midnight. He was going on to Rome from Venice and we were leaving the hotel at 5.20 a.m. the next morning. The gondola came for us a little before time and Aladin, Kathleen and I reached the station in good time for our seven o'clock train. As we sat in the station restaurant who should appear but Mr. Yeomans. He had called at the hotel at 5.20 to find we had already set off so he took a gondola and came down.

Fig. 4.4. *Alexis Aladin in British army uniform, 1920. (Photo: Courtesy John Rylands University of Manchester Library, Special Collections)*

He loaded us with fruit, chocolate, magazines etc. and as were leaving asked, "Have you sent a telegram to your home?" Of course we had not but he took our addresses in England and Mother received a wire assuring her of our safety. He had a banker's address in Sheffield to which I wrote to thank him for his kindness to us but that was the end of our contact with the courteous Mr. Yeomans.

Not so with Aladin. As Kathleen and I were travelling 1st class Wagon Lits, our carriage during the day was a sitting room, so to speak, and Mr. Aladin called to take us for meals and for chats in between – chats on all sorts of interesting subjects. He was of the old fashioned school of those days – 47 years ago – who could not allow the women folk to pay their meals, and he absolutely refused to let us do anything about it during our journey from Venice to Paris. He was staying behind in Paris and we were going through to Calais and London so I remarked "Well, if as you say, you may be lecturing in Britain, I must give you the address of a second home where they are supporters of the Friends of Russian Freedom." I did not mention either their place of residence or their names.[7]

7. JRL, Box 42, ECN to Professor R. H. Freeborn, notes of a visit to Connie Nightingale by Freeborn in May 1967.

During his time in England prior to 1917, Aladin had made many friends in journalism, government, politics, business, academe, and amongst émigré Russians. Closest amongst the friends was David Russell [Fig. 4.5], a successful Scottish paper manufacturer and Presbyterian thinker.[8] He and Aladin met in 1916, probably through mutual acquaintances, Jonas and Vera Kellgren. Jonas Kellgren was the director of a sanatorium in Sweden which placed emphasis on physical therapy, calisthenics, tranquillity, and the open-air life. As a young man in poor health, Russell had benefitted greatly from this unconventional medical regime. Russell, Aladin, and the Kellgrens also shared an interest in spiritualism and psychic phenomena, an interest epitomised in these years by the Society for Psychical Research. This society, amongst whose early leaders was Henry Sidgwick, Professor of Moral Philosophy at Trinity College, Cambridge, strove to explain otherworldly experiences, viz. clairvoyance, hallucination, and the summoning of the dead, in scientific terms. Could such phenomena be regarded as aspects of consciousness not yet acknowledged scientifically? Much discussion amongst those interested was driven by books written by F. W. H. Myers.[9]

After their meeting on the Orient Express Connie and Aladin did not meet again until the following year. On leave from The Mount School, Connie was in London assisting a Greek delegation negotiating a new treaty after the Turks rejected the Treaty of Sèvres. These negotiations were abruptly cut short by the death of the leader of the Greek delegation. At the time Aladin was living at the National Liberal Club as a guest of the government while Connie was staying at the Ritz Hotel with the delegation. Though Connie's correspondence reveals that they dined together at the hotel only once, the implication that other meetings elsewhere took place is clear. She stresses Aladin's eagerness to alert the British to the

---

8. Sir David Russell (1872–1956), LL.D., St. Andrews University 1922, Fellow of the Royal Society of Edinburgh 1936, forward-looking Scottish businessman and philanthropist with broad interests in photography, antiquarianism, internationalism, and the occult. See Lorn Macintyre, *Sir David Russell: A Biography* (Edinburgh: Canongate, 1994).
9. See F. W. H. Myers, *Human Personality and Its Survival of Bodily Death* (London: n.p., 1903).

Fig. 4.5. *Sir David Russell. (Photo: Courtesy University of St. Andrews Library Special Collections, ms38515/15/124/035)*

famine in Russia; and taking his appeal to heart she helped organise a gift from The Mount School of £400 to be sent to Russia.[10]

Between 1921 and Aladin's death in 1927 an intense correspondence developed between the two. What was at first a trickle of letters became a torrent. At her death Connie left 725 of Aladin's letters, along with other materials of his which she had – diaries, press cuttings, articles, etc. – to the John Rylands Library in Manchester.[11] These letters form the basis of much that follows here.

After the meeting in London, and in spite of the obvious spark between the two, further contact was slow in coming. For one thing, in early 1921

---

10. JRL, Box 42, ECN to Professor R. H. Freeborn.
11. The John Rylands Library joined forces with the University of Manchester Library in 1972, becoming the John Rylands University of Manchester Library. It is now considered a part of the University of Manchester Library. The Alexis Aladin Papers are housed in forty-five big boxes. The letters are arranged as follows: Box 32 (1921–Dec. 1923), Box 33 (Jan 1924–July 1925), Box 34 (August 1925–July 1926), Box 35 (August 1926–July 1927).

Aladin was preoccupied by another meeting – again on a journey, this time a cross-channel steamer – with an attractive young American girl. This girl was the eighteen-year-old Clare Boothe, later the famous Clare Boothe Luce, playwright, editor of *Vanity Fair,* conservative politician, and American ambassador. Though in later life Boothe made light of her flirtation with Aladin, letters of the time from her to him (in the University of St. Andrews archives) reveal a mutual infatuation. A hectic correspondence followed their meeting on the ferry; they met again in Paris and at other glamorous destinations, and gifts were exchanged. But by late April, Clare's mother, though she did not entirely disapprove of Aladin, had spirited her daughter back to America. In June Clare wrote to Aladin from New York saying she had run away from home and was leading an independent life in the city. This proved to be a short-lived experiment. When she wrote again in July it was from Greenwich Hospital. She had had an operation – for "appendicitis" she later said, though murmurs of an abortion were in the air.[12] No evidence of further involvement between the two has come to light.

Aladin's letters to Connie reveal the range of their interests. Aladin read widely in religion, politics, history, literature, languages, philosophy, and the sciences, sharing with Connie his views on many topics and welcoming her replies. She was much taken by his love of Russia, transparent in his discussions of politics and literature, and in his admiration of Britain, the British Empire, and the British way of life. Over the years he shared much personal detail – about his family in Russia, his wife, stepdaughter, his brother, and sister, and about his common-law wife in England, Florence Spence, and later their son, also named Alexis. As Aladin's possible usefulness to either the British or Russian government declined throughout the early 1920s and his capacity for making money in business or as a journalist waned, Connie responded positively time and again to his appeals for money, as did David Russell. On the other hand, she brushed aside an invitation to join him in Paris. She also rebuffed his increasing familiarities: when the letters changed from addressing her conventionally as "Dear Miss Nightingale" to addressing her as "Dear Constance" or

---

12. Christian, pp. 161–75.

"My dear Constance"[13] she took it amiss, just as it was presumably at her initiative that he changed the end of his letters from "all my love" to "yours." Although he went so far as to broach the subject of sex, there is nothing in the extant letters to suggest anything other than a platonic friendship. There was a deep affection between them, that seems plain – indeed a spiritual and emotional bond – but Connie did not welcome intimacies beyond those endorsed by the conventions of her upbringing.

After Clare Boothe's return to America the correspondence between Connie and Aladin picked up, letters written in 1921 giving a good sense of the myriad topics they discussed. In matters of literature Aladin ranged widely, commenting confidently both about the ancient Greek dramatist Euripides and the nineteenth-century Russian novelist Tolstoy. In discussing leadership qualities, he cites Ulysses admiringly; in matters related to the art of writing he discusses the power and aptness of metaphor, simile, symbolism, and personification. He asks Connie to look over and correct the English of some of his translations of Russian poetry. To Connie's comments on "people who sit down to create characters and invent situations in fiction," Aladin replies "they do not 'create' or 'invent'. They get into a semi trance condition and the 'characters' come to them and speak or write through them" (12/17/21).[14] There is much about his state of mind and self-knowledge, his internal life, his identity (soldier or contemplative?) (5/12/21); about religion, repentance, purgatory, psychology, the sadism of the Inquisition (5/30/21); about science, about the situation in Russia, "Lenin in a new moderate mood" (6/30/21); about the devastation of the countryside, the famine, the millions of dead, the weakness of Kerensky (8/9/21); and about his own "unshaken faith in my country's future" (9/20/21).

Discussion of such topics continued over the next two years. Other subjects too came up: the sciences, "knowledge of the outside world," astronomy, comets, the speed of light, electromagnetism (2/25/23), the concept of "scientific work as imagination and intellect combined" (9/13/23). Religion,

---

13. JRL, Box 32: 1/29/23, 8/29/23.
14. Parenthetical dates of this form in the text indicate the letters are from Aladin to Nightingale and in JRL, Boxes 32–5.

philosophy, and mysticism provoke numerous exchanges. "Without mysticism religion is an impossibility; without mysticism spiritual experience is an impossibility" (12/13/22). Thus Aladin reports on meetings and lectures of The Quest Society,[15] lamenting the "hopeless intellectuality of our times and the almost holy craving for the notion of repentance" (3/23/23). He thanks Connie for her "magnificent appreciation of the present position of the Friends. I do agree with you in your sincere sympathy towards the fundamental principles of their Faith" (9/4/23). He studies the comparison between European and Egyptian beliefs, sending Connie articles he had written on "The Soul of Ancient Egypt" (5/31/23; 6/6/23).

In a more worldly vein he is a great believer in Britain and the British Empire: "Listen to something from a stranger, a stepson of the mother who spread her arms scarlet colored over the face of the globe . . . awaken in your heart the good natural pride in the Greatness of the Red Areas on the World's map" (3/16/23). This excerpt speaks to his admiration for Britain but also exemplifies the overblown style of much of his writing, a style which did nothing to persuade editors to publish his work. He writes of his futile attempts to find employment, of introductions to possible employers or colleagues, some encouraged by Connie (6/4/23). and of having to vacate his desk at the offices of Tudor Pole & Co.[16] but finding a place at Fitch & Son (9/15/23).[17] Both Pole and Fitch were friends from before the war and with Russell and Aladin shared an interest in psychic phenomena.

He visited David Russell in Scotland, but was reluctant to tell Connie where he might be in late July: "what to say about the end of July and my whereabouts? Needless to say, always a pleasure to see you. Only I have not the faintest idea. . . ." (7/6/23). Connie shared his delight in Nature, in mountains, rivers, trees, and flowers, on one occasion sending him violets, on another roses, acknowledged at once (4/19/22), on another white

---

15. The Quest Society's principal quest was for connections amongst science, philosophy, and religion.
16. At 61 St. James Street SW1, a prestigious address which Aladin would have enjoyed; for all his affiliation with the Peasant Party and lingering belief that the peasants were the future of Russia he couldn't resist the lure of the smart, himself described on one occasion as a "dandy."
17. At 66 Bishopsgate EC 2.

heather, to which he replied "your letter and white heather are equally beautiful" (9/17/23). He followed his letter by a visit to York to lecture at The Mount School (10/2/23); the title of his talk was "The Peace of Christ in the Soul of the Soldiers."

On December 23, 1923, his situation changed dramatically with the birth of a son. The mother, Florence Spence, was a London housemaid.[18] The child, named Alexis after his father, but sometimes referred to as "Blue Eyes" or as "Alec," appears repeatedly in Connie and Aladin's correspondence. A month after his birth Aladin was already referring to his son as "Blue Eyes": "Blue Eyes grew a wee bit fatter, a great deal more observant."[19] Connie saw the boy for the first time when he was just a week old and agreed without hesitation to be his English godmother.[20] Aladin himself was having a difficult time, no longer welcome at the National Liberal Club, short of money, without a job, and living in a cramped bedsitter in Hampstead. He worried about "the mother" and the child, and renewed his pleas to Connie and to David Russell for money. They obliged. Despite his difficulties, he continued his reading and writing, often in the British Museum Library. As his exploration of mysticism went ahead, he wrote to Connie of "the road to mysticism" being prayer and love and "service in life to one's fellow men and women." He recommended Evelyn Underhill's book on "Man and His Relationship to Reality" to her, and to David Russell he proposed the establishment of a Chair of Mysticism at St. Andrews University.

His applications to the Foreign Office and the War Office for work as liaison to Russian officials were turned away, as was his appeal for help to Grand Duke Kirill Vladimirovich and other exiled Russians. Nonetheless, October found him in Prague – Connie and David Russell having agreed to care for Florence and his son in his absence – attempting to persuade Czech authorities to set up a Cossack and Peasant Bank, an enterprise that came to nothing.[21] During his two months in Prague, he wrote almost daily

18. Christian, pp. 192–4.
19. SAUL, AA to ECN, January 23, 1924, ms385515/7/4/1.
20. JRL, Box 42, ECN to R. H. Freeborn, July 1967.
21. A follow-up excursion to Bulgaria in search of paper contracts, funded by David Russell, likewise drew a blank.

to Connie. How she could shoulder the responsibility of keeping an eye on Florence and young Alexis at the same time as taking up her new appointment as Head of Dr. Williams' School, Dolgellau (formerly Dolgelley; see Chapter 5), in the autumn of 1924 is hard to imagine. Aladin congratulates her on her new appointment (9/8/24) but says not a word about the additional worries that care for his dependents imposed. By New Year's Day he was back in England, empty-handed.

In the early months of 1925 Aladin worked on other schemes, one for arranging closer contacts between American and Russian farmers, and another for acquiring properties in Czechoslovakia where Russian exiles could be trained for agricultural work after their hoped-for return to Russia. To set up these programmes he asked David Russell for £600 for travel to America, Paris, Prague, and Rome. Russell demurred, urging patience.[22] Meanwhile, his voracious reading in philosophy and science continued, focusing on the pre-Socratic Greek philosopher Heraclitus. Though no money was coming in, he declined small fees for translation or literary reference work, relying almost exclusively on what he termed "enclosures" (of money) from Connie and David Russell: "deepest thanks for enclosure, as usual it saved me in the nick of time" (10/18/25); another letter arrived with enclosures in November (11/7/25); and four more came the following month (12/17/25). Religion and politics continue as topics of interest: "you are perfectly right – my angry words about Lloyd George's form of delivery in his last speech are entirely out of place – mea culpa!" (10/14/25). It is worth noting that the wife of the Prime Minister, Dame Margaret Lloyd George, had been a pupil at Dr. Williams' School, as had her daughter Olwen Elizabeth Lloyd George.[23] That Connie's view of Lloyd George's speech was influenced by the family's connection to Dr. Williams' School is highly unlikely; that she shared Lloyd George's Liberal politics is much more probable.

---

22. Christian, pp. 203–4. Note that £600 in 1925 is equivalent in 2021 to £37,417.77 or US $51,474.26.
23. In June 1917 Olwen Lloyd George had become Olwen Lady Carey Evans, wife of Major Sir Thomas John Carey Evans, and later would be the grandmother of the Canadian historian Margaret Macmillan.

Connie's constitution was not the strongest, and she clearly felt the strain of her first year as Head of Dr. Williams' School. Aladin writes, "I am so pleased to hear you are by now with your friends who can arrange for you some real rest and recuperation" (8/12/25); "glad to hear you are improving and getting stronger" (8/22/25); "as you are having a heavy time" (10/8/25); "sorry to hear you are not well" (11/9/25). These references to Connie's poor health are often countered by happy recollections of meetings or anticipation of others: "your flying visit to London was a substantial help and support to your friend" (11/15/25); "next Thursday at 2 p.m. at Paddington I'll see you in London, that is unexpected and most excellent" (12/1/25). Later in the month however the gloomier tone is back: "since your departure all goes worse" (12/7/25). Occasionally Aladin begins his letter, "Dear Cony" or "Dear Tony." Whether these new styles of address carry implications is debatable, but whether or not, he broaches the matter of sex openly: "Today the spirit moves me to touch the question of sex" (10/26/25). He cites philosophers and churchmen: from Saint Clement of Alexandria, for example, ". . . when two shall be one." And "we go towards Astarte, Venus, Aphrodite, we are all children of god, the question arises what do we know, or can we know of the Way?" Follow-up letters explore "the essence of union as divine" (10/27/25) and wonder whether separation and abstinence may also be thought of as "divine" (10/28/25).

He writes of his business efforts, for instance, in tobacco (1/14/26), and of politics, notably a long defence of Mussolini in reply to Connie's objections "to the man and his methods" (11/14/26). He had some success with his writing: in April he reported for the *Daily Express* from Paris on a conference on "Russians Abroad," and in October four articles by him on the political situation in Russia appeared in the *Morning Post*. But he was always hard up, continuing to rely on "enclosures" from David Russell and Connie (1/29/26). In June he wrote a weary, self-indulgent reply to a letter from Connie which had hurt him: "your letter struck a very deep wound in my soul." Whatever the gist was, the flow of "enclosures" did not slacken: two instances in October (10/12/26; 10/24/26), three in November (11/15/26; 11/20/26; 11/22/26), and one in December (12/1/26).

Anxiety about health is seldom far away: towards Christmas of 1926 he writes, "your letters show that you were not quite well, what is the real position of your health? Is it serious?" he asks, and complains about his own ailments: "poorly, no appetite," "pain in back, did Swedish gymnastics" (11/16/26). After Christmas, a fit of depression is lifted: "moment of light, postman brought letters from you, one from Dolgelley advising your arrival, and two from Burnley" (12/27/26), where Connie had spent Christmas with her mother. Aladin mentions his boy's illnesses too. In September now nearly three years old, he had been "very ill with tonsillitis after inoculation against diphtheria" and was treated with a "heavy dose of iodine" (9/14/26). Though ill again later from "bronchitis" (9/23/26), he recuperated: "better on the 27th" (9/27/26). But the boy's illness was slow to release its grip: "Alec a wee-bit better" (9/30/26). His education also was a matter for concern. Connie asked Aladin's views about schooling, to which he replied, "your long letter and questions about private school. Personally, I never liked private schools, even the best." Shortly before Christmas the proud father reports that his writing was coming along nicely: "Alec wrote a letter to Connie with the help of his mother" (12/14/26).

During the last months of 1926 and the first six months of 1927 Aladin's health, plagued with arthritis, headaches, and intestinal pains, deteriorated, not helped by the dismal Hampstead flat in which he and his family lived. Despite his frailty, he went on reading and writing, even summoning enough strength to attend the opening of the Royal Academy Exhibition in January. Though his letters continue their range of interests, on world religions and his view of Christianity, for example, they concentrated also on his young son. He reported to Connie of his conversations with Alexis on "the Andersen stories" about "Jews" (i.e., "The Jewish Girl") and "The Stork," and mentions that he managed with considerable effort to take him on outings to Kew Gardens and Hyde Park (3/27/27, 3/28/27).

In rejecting the theory of original sin, he wrote of Jesus that he "would like to follow in his steps of a Joyous, Creative life whatever the end of it, and let the Semites and their miserable Christian imitators batter their heads, hearts and souls with Sin and Atonement" (4/14/27). Was he aware that his life was coming to an end? Connie continued sending him money; and in May he acknowledged a gift from her of a "pretty bag and the brooch" for Florence (5/22/27). But he was getting weaker, and a month later at his doctor's urging he entered St. Thomas's Hospital. The following day he wrote to thank Connie for a gift of "money" (6/21/27), and from then on wrote to her almost daily. The operation he had was serious, but he managed to keep up his interest in world events, mysticism and philosophy, renewing his study of Heraclitus. Connie kept sending him gifts – flowers, grapes, chocolates, cakes, etc. – but his time was running out. He died, following a second operation, on July 30. He was just fifty-four years old. In his last letter to Connie, he made an appeal for young Alexis: "poor kid . . . a little gentleman is crumpled up in him that would survive whether I help him or not, but if not helped in time, embittered, gone inside, indeed crumpled up" (7/22/27).

All the letters cited above were written by Aladin to Connie. I have come across only one of hers to him, from July 1923.[24] Aladin had written to her about a visit to Scotland at the invitation of David Russell, about the rejuvenation that he felt at Russell's friendship, about the glories of the Scottish countryside, and about the soul-searching he was suffering "chained in the world of time and space, in the fleeting moment of the flow eternal." Her reply is couched in even more high-flown language: "under the fostering guidance of the Lordly Ones . . . you have passed through the shadows and emerged into the bright clear radiance again – the natural atmosphere of a true follower of Ra!"[25] Connie followed this reference to Egyptian religion with a question: "Do you remember that old – old-fashioned perhaps to some – book of R. A. Vaughan, where in the final chapter of *Hours with the Mystics* the Flame-King appears showing all the creations of Fire. Then he gives place to King Sunlight who cries, 'with my shining in thy heart every flinty obstacle shall furnish thee with new fire. Shall it be then the splendour of the Flame God or the inward sunshine?'"[26] After expressing her bafflement at other parts of his letter, she turns from his state of mind to her own: "Lately I have been tortured and disturbed in soul. Perhaps in body, perhaps in soul. I know not. I overdid things preparing a lecture on 'Dreams' and had no chance of reserving my strength in other

---

24. SAUL, ECN to AA, July 5, 1923, ms8515/7.
25. Ra was the ancient Egyptian sun god, king of the gods.
26. Robert Alfred Vaughan, *Hours with the Mystics*, vol. 2 (London: Parker & Son, 1856), p. 331: "With my shining in thy heart, every flinty obstacle shall furnish thee with new fire. . . . Shall it be the splendour, or the inward sunshine?'"

directions. Naturally now that it is over, reaction comes and the inevitable loneliness of spirit."

This exchange of letters captures the otherworldly nature of much of their back-and-forth over the years: deeply personal, concerned with the life of the spirit, and marked by interest in theosophy, mysticism, folklore, magic, science, and psychology. It records their thoughts on worldwide consciousness, individual ecstatic experience, and the fallibility of human nature. These intellectual pursuits need not obscure the profound emotional bond they shared.

Respectful obituaries appeared in leading British newspapers. On August 3, 1927, the *Morning Post* stressed Aladin's deep knowledge of contemporary Russian affairs. Two days later *The Times* paid particular attention to his consistent support for the Allies during the war. The *Manchester Guardian* (August 6) regretfully noted the difference between his boundless activity before the war and his failing energy after the triumph of Bolshevism. As his hopes dwindled for a future Russia in which the peasant population would play the central role, and in which he himself would be a leading figure, he became more and more despondent.

After his death immediate problems facing his friends were his burial, his estate, and, above all else, what was to become of the three-and-a-half-year-old Alexis and his mother, Florence. By far the greater part of these cares was to fall to Connie and David Russell. Aladin was buried in Brookwood Cemetery (sometimes known as the London Necropolis) near Woking in Surrey. After lengthy discussion between Russell and Connie, a design for the headstone of the grave was decided, the work commissioned, and the headstone itself paid for by Russell. At the same time considerable expense was incurred by Connie. She settled Aladin's debts – the rent on his Hampstead flat, the rent of storage space in Southampton for things acquired during his time at Moonbeams Ltd., and debts incurred by Florence. Connie also took care of the continuing living expenses of Florence and the young Alexis.

But what was to become of them? Since Florence had said she wanted to train as a nurse, Connie made enquiries at several hospitals, to no avail. She also contacted more routine employment agencies who, equally, did not find Florence's credentials persuasive. Wanting to remove them from their dingy Hampstead flat, Connie made enquiries about homes for children "whose parents are abroad," and wrote to her sister Kathleen and her husband, the Rev. Jock Stedmond, to see if they could help. Writing to David Russell on August 8 she was apprehensive about the cost of a home for children in Bexhill which had been recommended, but the following week (August 15) was able to say that her sister and brother-in-law had agreed to give Florence and Alec a home. At about the same time she received a letter from Florence asking for money.[27] This prompted her to mention to Russell misgivings about various sums of money she had given Aladin over the course of the year, including £100 on March 28.[28] She was clearly implying that Florence had got hold of the money, and in the same letter suggested that Florence should be induced "to keep accounts, settled bills and so forth." On the day after this letter was written, Connie, Florence, and her son left London for Southampton and were welcomed into Jock and Kathleen's home.

Meanwhile there was discussion about how to secure the young boy's future. In the week following Aladin's death a blueprint for an Alexis Aladin Memorial Appeal signed by E. Constance Nightingale, W. Tudor Pole, and David Russell was prepared. Connie immediately wrote a cheque for £100 and sent it to Russell, promising a further £1,700 if Alexis's education continued until he was twenty-one. But the response from others consulted about such an appeal's prospects was discouraging. After much fruitless correspondence and discussion, Connie's patience ran out. Writing to David Russell on August 21 she declared:

> Personally, do you know what I would like to do? And I hope you will allow me to do it. I should like to contribute 200 pounds a year. It would not hurt me to do so. My future is assured.... So, please, Dr. Russell, expect another cheque for 100 pounds on January 1st and 200 pounds a year in the future. Poor old Aladin, he would hate publicity so very much and the response I fear would be very slight. Do not worry that the sum seems large. Believe me, it is small. If it did not go in that direction, it would be used in another and at thirty-five I do not need to hoard for my old age! So please

---

27. SAUL, FS to ECN, undated, ms38515/5/96/2. Connie is addressed as "Tonie," a name sometimes given her by Alec. The tone of the letter is polite but blatant.
28. SAUL, ECN to DR, August 21, 1927, ms38515/5/96/2.

let us close the appeal and do not ponder over the seemingly quixotic generosity. My salary is large and my needs small. You and Major Tudor Pole have establishments, families and all sorts of other calls so cannot quite realise that my contribution is nothing. I am so tired of talking money. It wearies me more than anything else. So allow me to do this.[29]

In Southampton, the first few days in the vicarage passed off without difficulty; as long as Connie was there, things went well. Alexis (now more often called Alec) settled easily, pleased to have the Stedmonds' daughter, Doreen (also aged 3), for a companion. Florence seemed content, provided that no demands were made on her. However, shortly before Connie was due to leave, Florence approached her, again asking for money – as if it were hers by right and as if Connie's generosity were boundless. Connie did not take kindly to this.[30] During a weeklong stay at the vicarage, differences between the Stedmonds' lifestyle and Florence's became more and more apparent to her, one example of which was the rights and wrongs of offering "sweets" (candy, toffees) to the children: Kathleen and Jock rarely provided such treats for Doreen, whereas Florence could hardly pass a sweet shop without "spoiling" Alec.

The situation deteriorated rapidly until Connie, picking up on dissatisfaction hinted at by Kathleen, asked for a candid assessment of the situation. Speaking for both, Jock replied at length in a letter.[31] He started by saying that if he or Kathleen was present, Alec "was developing well in every direction," adding, however, that these developments "fall away" if Florence was in the room. Acknowledging that the positive aspects of Florence's character would be known to Connie, he then drew up a list of what Kathleen and he saw as Florence's failings. She does not understand how dependent she is on others; she spends recklessly on unnecessary items; she incurs debts which are never paid; she buys trashy novelettes when Jock's library is available to her; she seldom bathes either herself or Alec; she leaves Alec's underclothes in tatters, remarking to the maid that "she cannot be bothered to darn like Mrs. Stedmond." She lacks any ideal:

---

29. SAUL, ECN to DR, August 21, 1927, ms38515/5/96/2.
30. SAUL, ECN to DR, August 30, 1927, ms38515/5/96/2.
31. SAUL, JS to ECN, October 20, 1927, ms38515/5/96/2.

"happiness is to get, no matter how, all that is possible and to give as little as possible." She refuses to discipline Alec, allowing him behaviours of which the Stedmonds disapprove. Their values – thrift, hard work, cleanliness, good manners, generosity – are alien to her. Not seeing a "workable end" in sight, Jock suggested that it might be wise "to bring the current arrangement to an end." The letter makes clear that with the right kind of discipline Alec would flourish, but that now he was allowed "to do and say things when alone with his mother which are not allowed when we are present."

Faced with this difficult situation, Connie sent a copy of Jock's letter to David Russell, adding that she thought it was time to give up on Florence, that she could not understand "her neglect of the boy to that degree." She would try to arrange for Alec to come and live with her in Dolgellau, at the same time making it clear to Florence that she must find a job in London.[32] A week later she was able to write, in happier vein, that the Chairman of the Governors of Dr. Williams' School had agreed to her "receiving Alec as a member of the school boarding establishment for the next few years." The Chairman also said he thought the governors would not "accept any fees from us," adding that all other expenses would be left to them – clothes, holidays, help needed when Connie was away, a maid to take care of his bath or, as she wrote wryly, "he might be neglected by his godmother!" She felt the responsibility deeply but took comfort in the knowledge that Russell was ready to help. On the 23rd of November 1927 she was able to write again that Alec had arrived in Dolgellau and was "safely installed here."

A new chapter was about to begin in his life, and in hers.

---

32. SAUL, ECN to DR, October 25, 1927, ms38515/5/96/2.

CHAPTER
5

DR. WILLIAMS' SCHOOL, DOLGELLAU

A Welshman by birth, Daniel Williams (1643–1716) at an early age showed an unusual aptitude for preaching. He was an obvious candidate for the ministry. Unwilling, however, to subscribe to the Act of Uniformity (1662) which required all church officers to adhere strictly to the regulations of the Church of England, he was soon identified as a Dissenter and was therefore unwelcome in the established church. Yet his situation took a turn for the better in 1664 when he became chaplain to the Countess of Meath. He remained in Ireland for twenty-three years, a persuasive preacher, a fierce opponent of Catholicism, and a sturdy nonconformist. Moving to London in 1687, and taking his views and his eloquence with him, he soon became a leader of the Dissenters in England. On his death he left £50,000 to charity: for the establishment of apprenticeships, for the foundation of elementary schools, one in England and others in Wales, and for a library the core of which should be his own collection of more than seven thousand theological books. This library is currently located in Gordon Square, London, and known today (2021) as Dr. Williams's Library.[1]

A century and a half after Dr. Williams's death Parliament, by the provisions of a new Education Act (1870), took control of all elementary schools in the country. This caused Dr. Williams's Trustees to close the schools, excepting only the school in Wrexham, Dr. Williams's birthplace. At the

---

1. In this chapter I have drawn from time to time on Merfyn Wyn Tomos, *"Honour before Honours": The DWS Story* (Bala, Gwynedd, Wales: Nereus, 2009). I have also profited from the wealth of material on the website of group of former students, the DWS Old Girls Association, https://www.dwsoga.org.uk/.

same time the Trustees decided to set up a nondenominational school for girls in North Wales with trust funds available from the closing of the other schools. They offered an endowment to Caernarvon (the most prestigious county town in North Wales; now spelled Caernarfon) provided that the town donate two acres of building land and supply a further £1,000. When Caernarvon was unwilling to meet these conditions, the Member of Parliament for the adjacent county of Merioneth, Samuel Holland, stepped in, suggesting Dolgellau as an alternative site. He personally stumped up the money to buy two acres of land and helped raise a further £1,000-plus locally. With the blessing of the Charity Commissioners, the Governors of the School met on September 15, 1875, for the first time, Samuel Holland in the chair. They were then ten in number: six representing the Trustees and four representing the Dolgellau School Board. Six were men and four were women. The school was ideally situated close to the River Wnion, the largest tributary of the River Mawddach, in glorious hilly countryside overlooked by the mountain Cader Idris.[2] Having welcomed its first pupils in 1878, the school was soon recognised for its academic rigour and its pioneering spirit.

In 1923, Florence Anstey, long-standing and highly respected Headmistress of the school, was looking forward to a well-earned retirement. Simultaneously the governors had begun the search for a successor. No fewer than fifty-five candidates applied for the post. Many were well qualified and experienced, but one stood out for her academic and international experience, her interest in girls' and women's education, her advocacy of education as a humanising experience, her rejection of traditional disciplinary methods, her vision, and the strength of her character: Ellen Constance Nightingale (B.A. 1913, M.A. 1914, University of Manchester), who came to Dr. Williams School from teaching at The Mount School, York, a Quaker school for girls, after years at other schools – a woman who had assisted at the Paris Peace Conference, worked on the Greek newspaper *Proodos* in Constantinople, and participated in refugee relief work.

---

2. In myth, Idris was a giant and early king of Merioneth, and Cader was his seat: the mountain has two peaks with a saddle, his seat, between the peaks. Hence the name Cader [Chair of] Idris.

1924–1928

The moment Connie Nightingale arrived in Dolgellau it was clear that a fresh chapter was opening in the life of Dr. Williams' School [Fig. 5.1]. Tall, dark-haired, and young (just 31), as Miss Nightingale entered a room her presence commanded attention. Her face was friendly and open, her gaze steady with a hint of twinkle in the eye [Fig. 5.2]. She looked different: her clothing – the long, simple dresses traditionally worn by head teachers of the time – was, contrary to custom, trimmed with silver braid and other discreet ornament, which caught the eye of style-minded students.[3] Altogether her appearance suggested change, difference, something out of the ordinary. As one former student later commented:

> [T]here was a glamour about Miss Nightingale, not of the Hollywood kind, but an elusive mysterious quality enhanced for us by her associations with the magic-sounding Istanbul, by shelves stacked with books by Russian authors, by strange slightly foreign looking coats and hand-woven jackets, and by the possession of an idyllic dream-cottage in the hills where, as privileged sixth formers, we were sometimes allowed to spend long summer days.[4]

Patterned with brightly coloured eastern motifs and probably acquired during her time in Constantinople, her shawls especially contributed to her faintly foreign aura. They hinted at a personality that too was different, and a will confident enough to introduce new policies to the school.

The most significant of these may have been in discipline. There was to be no more routine punishment. Connie did not allow the customary methods (detention, the writing of lines, and so forth) but replaced them with a new approach: talking quietly and persuading those in trouble to examine their conscience, consider the implications of their conduct (was it thoughtless or mean or plain wrong?), tell the truth, take ownership of what had happened, apologise, and make amends. Trust was all important – trust between girls and trust between staff and girls. She did not anticipate

---

3. Conversation with former (1933–5) DWS girl Vera (Gibbon) Lowe in Ripon, Yorkshire, July 17, 2017. I am most grateful to Vera for her help and hospitality.
4. Part of a memorial by Gaynor (Williams) Smith, DWS 1930–8, at the service for ECN at the Friends Meeting House, Euston Road, London, on February 29, 1968. Details of the London service were printed together with the programme of the memorial service held previously at Dr. Williams' School on January 31. On the "dream-cottage," named Ty Newydd, see pp. 71–3 below.

Fig. 5.1. *Dr. Williams' School in the 1930s. (Photo: Courtesy Dr. Williams' School Old Girls Association)*

misbehaviour. She expected the girls to conduct themselves honestly and respectfully, and to expect good behaviour of one another. Given the high level of classroom chatter and noise, normally restrained by threat of punishment, some of the teachers did not take kindly to the new disciplinary policy – and perhaps some of the girls did not either – but it took hold, and within a few months had changed the tone of the whole school. Some inkling of this change can be seen in the comments of two Old Girls:

> After spending 9 years of school life under Miss Anstey's strict disciplinarian rule, I was fortunate to come under Miss Nightingale's remarkable influence for twelve months, for which I shall never cease to be thankful. I hope I was perceptive enough for some grain of her spiritual influence to have rubbed off on me.[5]

5. Extract from Gaynor Smith's unpublished "A Patchwork of Memories," quoting another former student, available from the DWS Old Girls Association website, https://www.dwsoga.org.uk/assets/users/nestawynn@gmail.com/upload/Miss%20Nightingale.pdf, accessed July 18, 2021.

Fig. 5.2. *Connie Nightingale, Headmistress, 1924–40.*
(Photo: Courtesy Dr. Williams' School Old Girls Association)

Another, Gladys Dutton, recalls a time when she ran away from school:

> People were looking for me. I was scared during the night, was calling out and eventually was found. I thought I was really in for it and would be severely punished. Miss Nightingale instead made tea and had me sit with her. She told me how disappointed my parents would be with me and in a very calm voice talked with me for a long while. That was the end of it! Nothing more was ever said of the incident. What an amazing woman she was, and I learned so much from her that helped me in life.[6]

6. Excerpt from an interview with Gladys Dutton recalled on the Old Girls Association website, "Random Bits and Pieces from Gladys Dutton," https://www.dwsoga.org.uk/article-stories/random-bits-and-pieces-from-gladys-dutton-71732, accessed July 18, 2021.

This spiritual influence was rooted in the new head's personality, itself buttressed by Quaker values and practices. Such values have a long history in this part of Wales, finding precursors in the seventeenth-century Quakers living in and around Dolgellau. Many of these Welsh Quakers – hounded by the Catholic and Anglican churches barely a generation after their conversion to Quakerism in 1657 under the guidance of George Fox himself – were so strong in their convictions that they abandoned their homes, crossed the Atlantic, and founded a new settlement in Pennsylvania. They called this community Bryn Mawr, after the name of their leader's farm near Dolgellau.[7]

Connie Nightingale held to Quaker beliefs throughout her adult life – belief in the presence of God in everyone whatever their status, nationality, colour, or gender; belief in the community of all humans; belief in trust, respect, responsibility, truth, and honesty; belief in a simple life, and the blessing of silence. And it was these values she brought so influentially to bear and spread so meaningfully when she became Head of Dr. Williams' School in Dolgellau in 1924. It is reasonable to conclude that she thought the inculcation of these beliefs in the young – what she perhaps considered the way to "the good life" – was as meaningful a part of education as instruction in literature or science or the arts. She led her life according to these beliefs and taught the girls at Dr. Williams' School, as much by example as anything else, how to lead theirs.

At the same time as she encouraged the girls in the rights and wrongs of conduct, she was engaged in the day to day running of the school. Aside from the curriculum, class size, staff salaries, and so forth, there was the question of ensuring the school's success. This might be measured in various ways: growth in student numbers and in staff numbers, results of examinations, an expanding curriculum, the variety of sports opportunities, access to music and musicians, and most visibly in the construction of new

---

7. This leader was Rowland Ellis. For a lively take on these early Dolgellau Quakers see the historical novel by Marion Eames, trans. Margaret Phillips, *The Secret Room* (Swansea: Davies, 1975). Eames attended Dr. Williams' School during 1932–7. The Quaker college for women set up at Bryn Mawr, Pennsylvania, in 1885 (switched to nondenominational in 1893) is today amongst the preeminent liberal arts colleges in America.

Fig. 5.3. *Tremhyfryd and hockey field. (Photo: Jennie Forrester)*

buildings. Without hard evidence of planning, we cannot state for sure how Connie wished to proceed in these matters, but we can see from the historical record what developments took place, and draw conclusions.

She encouraged the enrollment of daygirls from the beginning, laying emphasis on the local character of the school. On her arrival there were forty-seven daygirls in school (alongside 129 boarders). Supported by an expanded programme of bursaries the numbers of daygirls doubled during her headship. In 1927 a Junior School for girls between the ages of 7 and 11 was opened at Tremhyfryd, a substantial stone-built house close to the school's main buildings [Figs. 5.3, 5.4]. Other marks of the new head's enthusiasm for local emphasis were the increased use of the Welsh language in the school, more articles in Welsh in the *School Magazine* than before, and more articles about Wales and the Welsh. The school's annual Eisteddfod was celebrated with more poems, declamations, and plays in Welsh. A Welsh Society, to organise relevant talks, visiting speakers, and trips, was also a notable startup.

As the numbers of daygirls increased, more classroom space was needed. This necessitated the adaptation of some dormitory space for classroom use and a consequent reduction in the number of boarders. More space was then needed if potential new boarders were not to be turned away.

Alert to this problem, and the need for funds to support new construction, Connie looked in the calendar for an event which could be the focus of an appeal. The school's Golden Jubilee, which would take place in 1928, offered as good an opportunity as any.

With fundraising aspects of the Golden Jubilee in mind, other significant developments between 1924 and 1928 can be recognised. The Old Girls Association, established at the turn of the century and best known for its biennial reunions and its publication of the *School Magazine*, offered a means of communication between past and present members, a reservoir of unwavering support and a vehicle for fundraising. It was now, with Connie's encouragement, galvanised into action. Organised into local branches, of which the London branch was preeminent, it set about preparations for the Jubilee and began raising money. A Loan Fund of £500, of which the recently (1925) founded Cardiganshire branch alone gave £100, was raised for Old Girls in difficult circumstances, and a further £50 for a Jubilee gift for the school. As news of the Old Girls Association and its activities spread, it expanded – a Merioneth branch was set up in Dolgellau in 1927 and another in Caernarfonshire and Anglesey the following year.

With the energetic renewal of the Old Girls Association went other initiatives. To involve the school in the wider world, Connie opened a branch of the League of Nations at Dr. Williams', and soon afterwards enrolled the girls in it one by one, thus endorsing the League and its principles. This involvement with the League went some way to balance the emphasis on Wales and the Welsh. Another innovation was the introduction in 1926 of "Parents' Weekend," an annual event at which parents, staff, and girls shared one another's company. The grounds and buildings were open to visitors; parents were free to take their girls out for meals if they chose; there was a religious service (nondenominational) and a concert. These weekends facilitated informal exchanges, helped cement relations between parents and the school, and spread knowledge of the school more widely.

With the approval of the school's governors. plans were drawn up for a construction project calling for a new wing with a gymnasium, more dormitories, and a new staff room; the alteration of the art room and a schoolroom into a new dining room, the old dining room becoming the new library; and the conversion of the hospital into a domestic science room.

Fig. 5.4. *Connie Nightingale on the steps of Tremhyfryd.*
(Photo: Courtesy Dr. Williams' School Old Girls Association)

The project was to be completed by the time of the Jubilee, and it was. On May 11, 1928, the day of the celebrations, the new wing was opened and the other alterations welcomed by the Duchess of Atholl.[8] The celebrations were marked by stage performances (including a short play by Connie herself); a ceremonial dinner attended by more than a hundred former students and all five former Headmistresses; and the presentation to the school by the Old Girls of gifts, including furniture for the head's room and the staff rooms. A religious service was held the next day at the school. The two-day event was a great success, a fitting salute to the school and the conclusion of the new head's first four years at the helm.

8. Parliamentary Secretary to the Board of Education, 1924–9, and Vice-President of the Girls Public Day School Trust, 1924–60. It is fair to assume that Connie met the Duchess in the course of her work for the Board of Education alluded to in correspondence between her and David Russell.

Personal Matters, 1926–1928

It was inevitable that news about Dr. Williams' School and the positive impact of Connie's headship should become widely known, so it was no surprise when other institutions tried to lure her away. On January 8, 1926, the General Committee of The Mount School, York (where she had taught classics from 1920 to 1924) interviewed candidates for the headship of the school. The committee concluded that Ellen Constance Nightingale "would if she had applied have been looked upon as the strongest candidate" and on that basis voted "unanimously to offer her the Headship."[9] Shortly after this meeting Connie visited York, as reflected in one of Alexis Aladin's letters: "hope earnestly that your visit to York helped you to formulate the problem and the Spirit led you to the right decision" (1/11/26).[10] Connie's decision to decline the offer is recorded in the minutes of the General Committee meeting on February 2.[11] More letters from Aladin in February suggest a second visit by Connie to the school, in all probability to explain her decision in greater detail: "by the time of this letter your York visit shall have been happily ended" (2/14/26), and "your York weekend a grand success and gave you satisfaction" (2/18/26).

Amongst other aspects of Connie Nightingale's personal life her involvement with Alexis Aladin looms large. What toll the stress of that relationship – for all the emotional support and intellectual pleasure she got from it – and his death took on her can only be imagined. She had agreed to be godmother to his child, so that after his death and in the absence of a sense of responsibility on the part of the boy's mother, she willingly shouldered the burden of caring for him. Within four months of his father's death the young Alec was living with her in Dolgellau [Fig. 5.5].

Correspondence between Connie and David Russell[12] then became frequent, often concerning the boy's well-being, but also addressing problems posed by his father's death, his papers, effects, memorabilia, and so on –

---

9. BIY, MOU 1/2/1/5, Minute Book 1910–27, p. 164.
10. The Aladin Papers (see Chapter 4, note 11) are a principal source for events in Connie's personal life between 1923 and 1927. Parenthetical dates indicate letters from AA to ECN; they are in JRL, Boxes 32–5.
11. BIY, MOU 1/2/1/5, Minute Book 1910–27, p. 165.
12. On Russell's friendship with Aladin see Chapter 4.

Fig. 5.5. *Connie Nightingale and Alexis Jr. shortly after his arrival in Dolgellau. (Photo: Courtesy Merfyn Wyn Tomos)*

there was no formal will. Their letters also ranged intellectually: both over questions of leadership and the quality of education, and over the intricacies of theosophy, spiritualism, mysticism, and states of consciousness, interests they had shared with Aladin. In a letter dated June 24, 1928, Connie writes that she was "conscious of Aladin these days"; he had died on July 30 the previous year. In another dated August 24 she remarks that "for Alexis' first birthday in the spirit world I sent some water lilies for his grave"; in yet another, discussing symbolism and quoting a letter Aladin had written her, she speaks of "the dark unclear powers." She mentions she is trying to arrange holidays for Alec with Florence, his mother, about whom the boy "never speaks," that Florence is in a good job, and (letter of October 14) that she is willing to adopt Alec but "I do not know whether his mother would consent." By December 4, Alexis is "very fit these days" but Florence is "without work."[13]

13. SAUL, ECN to DR, ms38515/5/96/2.

Continuing Success: 1929–1940

The school's growth in terms of student and staff numbers, student activities, and the provision of new facilities continued apace. By 1940, when Connie left Dr. Williams' School for the headship of The Mount School, York, the number of students had grown from 176 (47 daygirls) in 1924 to 295 (94 daygirls), and the staff had expanded from fourteen (of which two were visitors) to twenty. Though Connie's new approach to discipline had not been well received by all teachers at first, it is worth noting that half a dozen senior members of staff remained in post throughout her headship.

After the improvements made at the time of the Golden Jubilee there were no more building projects for a while. Activity resumed, however, in 1934 with the construction of a new entrance to the main building. And in 1935, in response to the growing student numbers and the need for more space, the governors authorised the purchase of a handsome house, Penycoed, on the slope of the hill above and behind the school the other side the main road. This house provided senior girls with lives of their own (hampered at first, it must be said, by the absence of electricity), though they had to walk up and down the hill from the house to the school, often in rainy and muddy conditions, and had to cross the road in the process. With the risks to the girls in mind, in 1937 Connie persuaded the governors to acquire fields either side the road to enable a bridge to be built over it. Completed the following year and offering a safe route between the main school and Penycoed, this footbridge was ceremonially opened by Dame Margaret Lloyd George, herself an alumna of the school[14] as part of the school's Diamond Jubilee celebrations.

The years preceding the Diamond Jubilee had presented the school with a serious challenge. Under criticism from the Board of Education and the Central Welsh Board, who were calling for more specialization in the curriculum, more facilities, more equipment, and more teachers, the governors decided that the current site was not fit for purpose: a wholly new school should be built elsewhere. This was easier said than done. When they found that in the difficult financial times (1936–7) they could not raise the

---

14. Wife of David Lloyd George (Prime Minister 1916–22), Margaret "Maggie" Owen from Criccieth had been one of the first boarding girls.

Fig. 5.6. *Dr. Williams' School, new hall and library, 1930s*
(Photo: Courtesy Dr. Williams' School Old Girls Association)

sums needed for such an ambitious project, they opted for another plan: they would extend and modify existing structures. A new complex, incorporating a spacious hall with stage and a library, was to be built [Fig. 5.6], with adjacent art, science, and domestic science facilities. Lord Howard de Walden[15] was on hand on June 24, 1939, to open this further evidence of the school's progress. Connie herself had played a leading role in the design of the hall, and was instrumental in persuading Edward Barnsley, the master carpenter, designer, and leading figure in the Arts and Crafts movement, to design and oversee the construction of the furniture for the hall and for the refurbished dining hall, as well as the provision of the beds and chairs for the dormitories.[16] The furniture well exemplifies Barnsley's

15. Thomas Scott-Ellis, 8th Baron, soldier, author, connoisseur, President of the Campaign for Protection of Rural Wales (1931–45), and Welsh speaker.
16. Edward Barnsley, also a Quaker, had doubtless become known to Connie through her friendship with the Gimson family and theirs with the Barnsleys; see Chapter 2. On Barnsley see Annette Carruthers, *Edward Barnsley and His Workshop: Arts and Crafts in the Twentieth Century* (Wendlebury: White Cockade, 1992).

lighter style, adding distinguishing notes to the school's appearance. It marked the school's alertness to contemporary developments in design and woodwork; in addition it underscored Connie's wish to point the girls towards a wider world of high intellect and aesthetic sense.

The school progressed in other ways too. Under the impetus of the Golden Jubilee the Old Girls Association expanded its activities and membership steadily: 1930 saw the first of the annual dinners at the school and 1931 the first London dinner. To the three already existing local branches others were added: Flint and Denbigh (1936), Montgomery (1938), and a "foreign" branch for those resident abroad in 1936. The overseas branch provides further evidence of Connie's interest in broadening the school's horizons, an interest marked also by the presence of visiting staff members from abroad every year and by her encouraging the girls – this in the context of their membership in the League of Nations – to write letters to girls in other countries all over the world, such as Sweden, Poland, France, and the United States. There were trips abroad too: an outing to Paris in 1935 was vividly remembered by Vera Gibbon, who describes the channel crossing in bemused terms: "I went up on deck. . . . it was a great deal better than those stuffy bunks. We were accompanied during our journey by a crate of croaking frogs. I tremble to think what they were doing on a ferry to France!" In Paris she recalls the places they visited, most notably the Louvre, Les Invalides, and the Opéra (for a performance of *Rigoletto*), a rewarding taste of European culture at first hand.[17] And in 1938 Connie herself and five other staff members took a group of thirty-one girls on a tour of Italy – and this at a time when political tensions between Britain and Italy were rising and Mussolini was at the height of his powers.[18]

Closer to home there were opportunities for bike rides into Barmouth and outings to the beaches at Fairbourne and Friog for picnics. In 1927 a group of girls journeyed to Criccieth to witness a solar eclipse. From 1929 annual arrangements were made for girls to attend meetings of the youth Eistedd-

---

17. Vera Gibbon, "My Life at DWS," Old Girls Association, https://www.dwsoga.org.uk/en/article-stories/my-life-at-dws-by-vera-gibbon, accessed July 15, 2021.
18. See Lawrence Dundas, *"Essayez": The Memoirs of Lawrence, Second Marquess of Zetland* (London: John Murray, 1956), 228, 262, 293. The Marquess of Zetland, a prominent landowner and politician, was Secretary of State for India, 1935–40.

fod, a festival of music and literature, at venues in various parts of Wales. Music was often the focus of other excursions: in 1932, for example, school orchestra members went to Aberystwyth to see a rehearsal by the University of Wales's Music Department of the opera *Hansel and Gretel*; later that year they attended a concert conducted by Sir Adrian Boult in Harlech. In 1936 seventy girls went to a music festival in Oswestry, where they joined with girls from two other schools in a massed choir concert performance.

Music, and choral music specially, has always played an important part in Welsh life. It has always featured prominently in the DWS curriculum: music theory, harmony, and choral music were taught from the very start. Building on this tradition Connie both encouraged vocal music and music theory, and vigorously supported the teaching of instrumental music, all of which led to the establishment of the first school orchestra. The crescendo of interest she generated resulted in the hiring of a second music teacher, with consequent development of the instrumental side. By 1930 there were no fewer than four orchestras representing the different age groups amongst the pupils, the senior orchestra playing at morning assembly every day. The absence of a high-grade piano was remedied in 1934 by Connie's acquisition of a 1780 Broadwood piano. And in 1939 the music staff raised the funds for a new organ for the new hall. The study of music and participation in musical events were integral to Connie Nightingale's concept of education.

The delight of many pupils in the school's approach to music is well described by an Old Girl, Vera (Gibbon) Lowe, who reminisces:

> A whole new world opened for me in a school noted for music. My previous music master, a very good man, and a good teacher, was our local church organist. His favourite music was therefore of that nature. I had Mendelssohn and Beethoven chosen for me by him. . . . At DWS all that changed. I had Miss Ingram to teach me there. . . . [She] allowed me to use her music cubicle, and any of her books of music, when I had spare time. I discover Chopin, Mos[z]kowski, several Spanish composers, ballet music and other music for dance. In other words, romantic music with feeling, worlds apart from church music, but for me it was a revelation.[19]

19. Vera Gibbon, "[My] Life at DWS," downloaded from https://www.dwsoga.org.uk/assets/users/suecarter100@gmail.com/upload/MYLIFEATDWSbyveragibbon.pdf, accessed July 19, 2021.

In conversation at her home in Ripon, Vera added how pleased she had been to be introduced to the Romantics. "Rachmaninoff!" she exclaimed. "Chopin!"[20]

Amongst extracurricular activities, gardening, soon formalised as a Young Farmers Club, remained popular, as did the gramophone club and the Literary and Debating Society. New were a bird watching/hiking club (1928), a chess club (1937), and an art club (1938). Sport commanded a good deal of attention and took a good deal of time. Hockey and netball took pride of place, followed by tennis. River bathing was added in 1929 for seniors. Calisthenics and gymnastics were regular activities. There were opportunities too for croquet, badminton, rounders, and horseback riding – and, believe it or not, cricket, a reminder of Connie's undergraduate days. The annual Sports Day crowned the year for the athletic, whereas walking was a year-round pastime, eagerly encouraged, for all.

Urged to appreciate the natural beauty around them – the woods, the rivers, the open countryside, and the hills – the girls were, within reason, allowed to come and go as they pleased. On Saturdays special arrangements for longer rambles came into play when groups of six girls (two seniors and four juniors) went off on their own, the seniors specifying to the staff member in charge where each group was headed. Many walks came to be traditional, of which three were popular: the Precipice Walk, which wandered along in the woods on the far side of the Dolgellau–Barmouth road; the Torrent Walk, clambering dangerously along the banks of tributaries of the River Mawddach; and the Cader Walk, roaming across the flanks and screes of the mountain itself.

Every year on a day that she thought suitable for a climb up Cader Idris Connie would announce a holiday. The whole school scrambled to change clothes, collect picnic lunches at the kitchen, and start off. It is a stiff climb. There are two routes, the longer but easier, and the shorter but more difficult, a breathless climb up the Fox's Path. Normal custom was to take the longer up, picnic on the summit – often wreathed in mist but offering spectacular views when clear – and take the quicker down, more of a slither-

---

20. Conversation with former (1933–5) DWS girl Vera (Gibbon) Lowe in Ripon, Yorkshire, July 17, 2017.

slide than a controlled descent. About halfway down the climbers passed a tarn where they paused for a drink.

Personal Matters, 1929–1940

Connie's correspondence with David Russell throws light on major aspects of her private life during this period, amongst them her concern for Alexis Aladin's reputation and the thriving of his son, Alexis Jr.[21]

Aladin's Reputation

Others' views of Aladin and their respect or lack of it for him varied over time. Recall that as a young man he was known for his eloquence and progressive views. Imprisoned in 1895 for nine months and sentenced to three years internal exile, he fled the country. Back in Russia ten years later he led the Peasant Party in the 1906 Duma, whose abrupt dissolution forced him into exile again. In England he was known as an Anglophile, and during World War I as an advocate for Anglo-Russian friendship. Many thought a promising political career was his for the taking; and there were times during the war when, sent back to Russia by the British government, it seemed he might again become influential in Russian politics. But his attempts to discover the intentions of Kerensky's Provisional Government failed, as did his approaches to General Kornilov. Suspected of plotting a coup against Kerensky's government in late August 1917, Kornilov and his associates, including Aladin, were arrested and imprisoned. Released in mysterious circumstances in November they made their way south into Cossack territory, where antirevolutionary White armies were assembling.[22] After fierce fighting in 1918–19 against the Bolsheviks, in which Aladin took part, in 1920 the White armies were defeated. Following their collapse –

21. SAUL, ms38515/7/4/1 (1922–7), ms38515/5/96/2 (1928–33), and ms38515/5/96/3 (1934–43).
22. George Katkov, *Russia 1917, the Kornilov Affair: Kerensky and the Break-up of the Russian Army* (London: Longman, 1980). Amongst more recent commentators Orlando Figes, *A People's Tragedy: The Russian Revolution 1891–1924* (London: Jonathan Cape, 1996) takes the view that, far from instigating a coup against Kerensky, Kornilov intended to bolster him by checking growing Bolshevik power.

and given the perception that he changed allegiances easily – Aladin came to be distrusted by both Reds and Whites. In England once more, any influence he had had in official circles waned rapidly, his reliability came to be questioned, and journalistic opportunities dwindled.

Reasons for Connie's concern for Aladin's reputation may be judged by Kerensky's view of him as outlined both in a 1934 talk at the National Liberal Club in London and in his book *The Crucifixion of Liberty*, where he described Aladin as a "soldier of fortune" and nothing more.[23] Similarly, Sir Bernard Pares, British military attaché to the Russian Army at the British Embassy in 1917, writing in *My Russian Memoirs* makes light of Aladin's contributions, underscoring the "'soldier-adventurer' atmosphere."[24] The slighting of his record continued.[25] Aside from his professional life, he was known as a mystic. Some thought him unsure in his beliefs and unpredictable, others that he was a dreamer and an opportunist. David Russell, hearing in the week after his death that Aladin had expressed his "doubts" to a friend, wondered whether Connie had heard of such doubts. Her reply was firm: such comments were "misunderstood"; true, he had "dark moments, but that did not shake his faith in Providence and an all-loving Father; odd remarks were made to me in the past week which tried to shake my faith in Aladin. Happily, I had knowledge to counter the effect, so I did not worry."[26] Influenced herself by spiritualism and curiosity about the unconscious, Connie attempted throughout her life to contradict negative views of Aladin.[27]

Alexis Aladin Jr. and Ty Newydd

Prominent amongst threads in Connie's letters to Russell is her concern for Aladin's son. After Aladin's death young Alexis (often referred to by her

---

23. SAUL, ECN to DR, March 14, 1934, ms38515/5-96-3; Alexander Kerensky, *The Crucifixion of Liberty*, trans. Gleb Kerensky (New York: John Day, 1934), p. 351.
24. SAUL, ECN to DR, April 30, 1935, ms38515/5-96-3; Bernard Pares, *My Russian Memoirs* (London: Jonathan Cape, 1931), p. 471.
25. Cf. Christian, p. 43, citing P. N. Milyukov, *Vospominaniya*, vol. 1 (New York: Chekhov, 1955).
26. SAUL, ECN to DR, August 10, 1927, ms38515/7-4-1.
27. Christian, pp. 226–8.

as "Alec") and his mother, Florence, went to live with Connie's sister Kathleen and her family, as we have seen (Chapter 4). When this arrangement proved unworkable, Connie arranged for Florence to return to London, where she found a job in mid-January, lost it through illness, but found another; and for young Alec to live with her in Dolgellau.[28] When Connie worried about his education and living arrangements, the school's governors stepped in. They let him be enrolled "for the next few years" as a boarder and waived all fees. At this difficult moment for Connie, one of her friends, Melita Alexander, who was staying with her at the time, exclaimed, "Thank heavens Dr. Russell is with you!"[29] In caring for Alec Connie was always helped by David Russell and his family, who shared the costs of his upbringing and provided a second home for him in Scotland. They took to him, Russell commenting how much they enjoyed having him stay.[30]

In 1929 Connie bought Ty Newydd, a handsome Elizabethan house (she called it a cottage) for herself and Alec on the approaches to Cader.[31] Stone-built, with an impressive gabled front porch, three dormer windows on the second floor making for comfortable if snug bedrooms, and two squat chimneys either end of the sloping roof, it nestles at the foot of the mountain with glorious views in every direction, the mountain standing bold behind the house. There is a grassy space, not exactly a lawn, in front of the house, and a garden at the back with a stream running through it. It was furnished in Connie's day (author's personal recollection) with old Welsh furniture – a dresser, settles, wooden chairs, stools, and chests, testifying again to her love for everything Welsh – and a very large fireplace in the sitting room. Set back from, and to the east of the house is another building used in modern times as a garage. Recent study of this structure, Ty Hyfryd, has shown that it too was a dwelling, earlier in date than Ty Newydd. Built on timber-frame cruck principles revealed in the lower

---

28. SAUL, ECN to DR, April 5, 1928, ms38515/5/96/2.
29. SAUL, ECN to DR, November 2, 1927, ms38515/7/4/1. Melita Alexander was sister of Sir Frank Alexander, Lord Mayor of London (1944–5).
30. SAUL, DR to ECN, October 7, 1933, ms38515/5/96/2: "We all liked Alexis. Anne and he, of about an age, were very special friends."
31. SAUL, DR to ECN, May 17, 1929, ms38515/5/96/2.

courses of exterior walls, it was probably the home of one of the first occupants of the site, perhaps as early as 1600 A.D.

The main purpose of Ty Newydd was to provide access to the countryside for both Connie and Alec, giving them both a change from the institutional atmosphere of the school. For Alec, who from an early age had shown, like his father, a liking for the natural world – flowers, animals, birds, insects, tadpoles, frogs, worms[32] – Ty Newydd and its immediate surround offered boundless opportunities for his wanderings. What is more, he had a bicycle to explore the lanes and hedgerows and was having riding lessons: Connie noted, "the groom says he will make a good horseman." For Connie Ty Newydd provided an undisturbed space for work and reflection, a home where she could entertain senior girls from school, and during the school holidays could look after students whose parents were abroad. At Christmas 1930 for instance, she took care of a group of three boys and one girl, and the following year told Russell that she "was writing from the cottage where my family of six children from abroad spend their holidays."[33] For both Connie and Alec, the cottage and countryside offered obvious benefits for their health – not always as robust as either might have hoped. In August 1930 Connie suffered a bad attack of rheumatism requiring a stay at a clinic near Hereford, and in late November she fell ill for six weeks with the flu.[34] Alec in 1933 suffered a bad attack of pneumonia, needing the help of a doctor and two nurses: Connie wrote, "there was a grim battle for a few days," and "he was terribly ill, but bright withal."[35]

Alexis's (Alec's) Education

Alec's education is discussed repeatedly, a topic lent context by Russell's concern for the education of his own boys, David (b. 1915) and Pat

---

32. A diagram of a "wormery" [sic] drawn by him is included in a letter from Connie to Russell. SAUL, ECN to DR, January 3, 1930, ms38515/5/96/2.
33. SAUL, ECN to DR, January 3, 1932, ms38515/5/96/2.
34. SAUL, ECN to DR, August 9 and November 12, 1930, ms38515/5/96/2.
35. SAUL, ECN to DR, April 27, 1933, ms38515/5/96/2.

(b. 1918). Russell asks Connie her views of Stowe School, about which he has heard good things. Connie agrees. She also mentions somewhat curiously, as suitable for Alec perhaps, a school in Derbyshire whose Headmaster has extraordinary psychic powers.[36] But Russell decides on Sedbergh School. where a friend, the Rev. Neville Gorton, was a housemaster.[37] "He will be better there than at Stowe." Connie voices her approval: "Sedbergh has a fresh air atmosphere in more ways than one."[38] Twelve months later she wrote: "Alexis works terribly hard. His brain is most active. Fortunately, he is strong physically and for a child of six can walk seven miles without raising a grumble. I think you will feel that he will repay all your care and generous thought for him. I should like to discuss his future with you, but I gather that you are content at present to leave him at our Junior School? It is a small class of four boys and five girls with an excellent mistress."[39] A year later, keeping "amazingly well," Alec sends a painstakingly written note – "Dear Uncle David, Thank you very much for the lovely present. With kisses from Alexis"[40] – and follows with a similar note in October. By year's end, nearly eight, he is "reading, growing enormously, and full of good spirits and excitement."[41]

Before long Connie writes to ask Russell's advice. She has thought Alexis could stay a while longer at the Junior School but now thinks he is ready for a move. She has visited a school highly recommended by several parents, Earnseat at Arnside in Westmorland, and liked the head and his wife. Alexis too liked them and is keen to go. She has reserved a place. Did he approve?[42] Replying, Russell recommends Cressbrook at Kirkby Lonsdale, where his younger son, Pat (at Sedbergh School with his brother, David) has been, fees the same as Earnseat, thirty-five boys, Headmaster Dowson

---

36. SAUL, DR to ECN, March 23, 1928, and ECN to DR, March 26, 1928, ms38515/5/96/2.
37. Gorton was later Headmaster of Blundell's School 1934–42 and Bishop of Coventry 1942–55.
38. SAUL, DR to ECN, March 19, 1929; ECN to DR, May 27, 1929, ms38515/5/96/2.
39. SAUL, ECN to DR, April 15, 1930, ms38515/5/96/2.
40. SAUL, ECN to DR, March 8, 1931, ms38515/5/96/2.
41. SAUL, ECN to DR, November 15, 1931; December 12, 1931, ms38515/5/96/2.
42. SAUL, ECN to DR, Whit Monday, May 16, 1932, ms38515/5/96/2.

"a man of high ideals, boys all love him, and his wife too." Just a suggestion, he prefers to leave the decision to Connie.[43] She chooses Earnseat, where, according to his end-of-term report, Alexis spent a good first term.[44] He evidently enjoyed school life, worked hard, did well at math, and kept busy; his school reports – which Connie conscientiously sent on to Russell – lament only his cavalier attitude to spelling.

One aspect of his education, foreign travel, was taken in hand by Connie herself. In the spring of 1935, she took him on a tour of Greece and the Aegean. Writing from Skyros on April 20 she comments: "The boat is small but the company good. We have had most interesting visits though the weather was too bad for landings at Perachora and Samothrace. Tomorrow we return to Sunion and then after Ithaca we go to Monaco and so home."[45] Alexis, writing to Russell, shows himself a keen observer of the archaeology and of nature:

> S. S. Velos TROY 17th April
>
> Dear Uncle David,
>
> We are having a marvelious [sic] time in Greece and the Islands are simply beautiful. Olympia was very nice but very hard to understand. The statues were very well preserved, but the buildings were all upside-down.
>
> Delphi was much nicer because you could see the buildings and imagine the people in them, in the museum we saw a lot of beautiful statues.
>
> We went to Priene and we saw all the buildings and and [sic] these are some of the buildings: – Gymnasium, Stadium, agora, and a very well-preserved theatre, and council chamber. There were a lot of inscriptions on the walls. I saw 8 huge eagles which were soaring above our heads – We could see the river Maeander and the sea beyond.
>
> On the way back to the port our stirring [sic] wheel broke and we had to walk about half an hour and a car picked us up.
>
> Troy was very nice, and we saw some ruins but not very good ones. We went to the museum which was very good.
>
> Well good by [sic]. I'll write again soon.
>
> Love from Alexis[46]

---

43. SAUL, DR to ECN, May 20, 1932, ms38515/5/96/2.
44. SAUL, ECN to DR, January 2, 1933, ms38515/5/96/2.
45. SAUL, ECN to DR, April 20, 1935, ms38515/5/96/3.
46. SAUL, AAJr to DR, April 17, 1935, ms38515/5/96/3.

On their way back they stopped in Paris, where Alexis's comment on the Louvre was: "I like the Victory statue very much but I'm very sorry I don't like the Venus of Milo."[47]

All his school reports were positive, as a few excerpts indicate: "capable of hard work"; "genuine capacity for enjoying other things"; "nature study well to the fore"; "not lacking in grit."[48]

The question of his next step, the move from prep school to public school, was in the air. Connie writes that she has met Donald Gray, Headmaster of Bootham School in York, and that he would like Alexis to go there "fairly young." She wonders whether Russell favours a move in September 1936 or 1937. "He was born December 1923," she reminds him.[49] Russell sent a thoughtful reply. He and his wife had inquired about Bootham School for David and Pat, and heard nothing but good about it. If Connie had confidence in the Headmaster and was satisfied about sending Alexis there, he would be entirely happy about her choice. He went on:

> When Pat was at Cressbrook, Mr. Dowson, the Headmaster, said that if he did not succeed in bringing a boy to realise what self-control meant and had acquired it in some degree before he left his school, he felt he had failed. He was also of the opinion that the development in the average boy is very marked between the ages of 12 and 14 – usually nearer 14 than 12 – and it is of some importance that a boy should have found himself and realised the meaning of independence and of self-control before he goes to his Public School. That anyhow is my feeling and I do not feel that age matters as much as the boy's development. Of that you are the best judge.[50]

Connie decided he should stay another year at Earnseat, during which he took and passed the exams for entry to Bootham. She comments that by the time he left Earnseat he had become "a great big fellow for his thirteen years."[51] He spent part of the September before going to Bootham with the Russells in Scotland, about which Russell says that he seemed "quite at home" and that Rev. Neville Gorton, who also visited for a few days,

47. SAUL, ECN to DR, April 25, 1935, ms38515/5/96/3.
48. SAUL, ECN to DR, August 14, 1935, ms38515/5/96/3.
49. SAUL, ECN to DR, December 5, 1935, ms38515/5/96/3.
50. SAUL, DR to ECN, December 21, 1935, ms38515/5/96/3.
51. SAUL, ECN to DR, April 17, 1937, ms38515/5/96/3.

was quite "struck with him." He adds that the family was "greatly pleased with Alexis."[52] A year later Connie wrote that he had settled well at Bootham, that their invitation for him to spend part of the Christmas holidays with them was very welcome, and that "she loves him to come to you more than anywhere else in the world though I hope he is not a trouble to you. He is a huge creature now. People offer him cigarettes thinking he is 19 instead of 14!"[53]

The Question of Legal Adoption

The question of the regularization of Alec's relationship to Connie remained. For all intents and purposes Connie had acted as surrogate mother to the boy from the moment in November 1927 that he came, at the age of 3 (almost 4), to live with her in Dolgellau. At once she began to think about making provision for him for the rest of his life, and within a year letters to David Russell show her interest in settling her insurance policy (£750 plus profits) and "other things" including an annuity on him, and her understanding that "it would be easier to do this if I adopted him which I am willing to do, but I do not know whether his mother would consent."[54] There seems to have been little further discussion on this topic until legal matters to do with his father's death – the absence of a will beyond his handwritten note (unwitnessed) leaving everything to Florence, letters of administration, and so on – came to the fore in 1931. At that point Connie wrote to Russell that "Alec's mother had suggested that I should adopt Alexis legally. I am quite willing to do so in order to protect his future which might become precarious as he approached wage-earning age of 14."[55] A year later the situation had not changed; she writes in answer to a question from Russell, "I have not yet drawn up a legal bond of annuity for him until we had our long-promised discussion on the advisability of my adopting him to avoid possible complications when he is older. In any

---

52. SAUL, DR to ECN, October 1, 1937, ms38515/5/96/3.
53. SAUL, ECN to DR, October 1938, ms38515/5/96/3.
54. SAUL, ECN to DR, October 14, 1928, ms38515/5/96/2.
55. SAUL, ECN to DR, June 30, 1931, ms38515/5/96/2.

case you are safe in claiming that he has no legal annuity other than yours."[56]

Some years later Russell writes, apologetically, "I promised a long time ago to inquire into the question of the custody of Alexis. I enclose a memorandum handed to me by Dr. Watt which I think you will consider entirely satisfactory."[57] The memorandum "in regard to the custody of Alexis Aladin [Jr.]"[58] addresses three main points: "the welfare of the infant" (by "infant" is meant anyone under the age of 21); "the rights of the parents"; and "whether the infant is of an age to exercise a choice." The third of these points may have been the most telling:

> Where the parent has allowed the child to be brought up by and at the expense of another person for such length of time and in such circumstances as to satisfy the court that the parent has been unmindful of the parental duties owed to the child, the court may not make an order for the delivery of the child to the parent, unless satisfied as to the fitness of the parent to have the custody, having regard to the welfare of the child:
>
> "Where an infant, who has passed tender years and is of a reasonable age, is out of a parent's custody, and desires to remain out of it, he will not be compelled to return to it, if his welfare does not so require."[59]

Connie considered this quite satisfactory and reasonable.[60] And we may assume that Alec did so too. It becomes apparent that Russell handled all legal questions relating to Aladin's death and the status of his son.

Iona and Other Involvements

Given her mother's Scottish connections and her own fondness for Scotland, the country had become more and more attractive to Connie. But other places also had their appeal: Connie and Alexis visited Greece in 1935, as we have seen, and Connie had visited previously in 1929 and

---

56. SAUL, ECN to DR, Whit Monday 1932, ms38515/5/96/2.
57. SAUL, DR to ECN, November 28, 1935, ms38515/5/96/3.
58. SAUL, David Russell Collection, file "Bonds of Annuity," ms38515/1/3/8.
59. Here "Bonds of Annuity" cites *Halsbury's Laws of England*, vol. 17, *Infants and Children*, p. 109, ¶256.
60. SAUL, ECN to DR, December 5, 1935, ms3815/5/96/3.

1932, either on her own or with Melita Alexander. She also visited Madeira in 1932 and Italy in 1938, keeping up her international connections. But Iona, an island off the west coast of Scotland – well known as the Scottish home of Saint Columba, then as a Benedictine community, and in the twentieth century as the centre of an ecumenical Christian community – always beckoned. When she left The Mount School in 1924 to take the headship of Dr. Williams', she was given as a leaving present a silver St. Martin's cross, emblem of Iona; the school gratefully declaring, she said, that "the lore of Iona had been so much a part of my contribution."[61] David Russell's involvement with Iona now brought home the island's significance in her own life.

Russell had initiated and paid for religious retreats for divinity students on the island in 1920. In 1929, under the vigorous leadership of the Rev. George MacLeod,[62] the retreats were incorporated into the newly formed Iona Fellowship, which in 1938 became part of the Iona Community. McLeod saw the community as committed to Christian values, peace, and social justice, and to the spiritual practices of prayer, song, and silence. He envisaged it as international in scope. Connie felt drawn to this fellowship and was enrolled by Russell in 1932. With his help she, Alexis, and Melita Alexander were able to visit for two weeks in September of that year, when Connie was delighted "to see more of Mrs. Russell and the family."[63] The Russell family regularly spent a four-week summer holiday on the island, where they were joined by Alexis as often as possible.

The increased visibility and success of Dr. Williams' School, meanwhile, did not fail to attract the attention of others. In 1929 Connie was offered the headship of a school in Scotland, which, despite her Scottish affinities and her mother's Scottish forebears, she declined. Local interest in her activities and her enthusiasm for all things Welsh was no less well recognised, so that two years later she was elected a member of the Council of the Uni-

---

61. SAUL, ECN to DR, March 23, 1932, ms36515/5/96/2.
62. George Fielden MacLeod (1895–1991), Baron MacLeod, soldier and clergyman, founder of the Iona Community, became, amongst other responsibilities gladly shouldered, Moderator of the Church of Scotland. See Ron Ferguson, *George MacLeod: Founder of the Iona Community* (Glasgow: Collins, 2001).
63. SAUL, ECN to DR, October 17, 1932, ms36515/5/96/2.

versity of Wales, an honour she accepted gracefully and cherished.[64] Her leadership qualities were also recognised at Westminster, where she was asked to serve on committees of the Board of Education; in 1934, for example, she made flying visits to London to attend monthly meetings of the subcommittee on Libraries in Secondary Schools.[65]

Her reputation as an educational leader had grown together with her sense of loyalty to the school and her affection for Wales, so that it seemed unlikely that she could be persuaded to take any other headship. But her popularity in Quaker circles in York; the recollection of her sympathetic teaching both at Bootham School during World War I and The Mount School thereafter; her firmness of purpose; and her reputation as a scholar and administrator made it certain that when an opportunity presented itself The Mount School would come calling again, as they had in 1926. So, as the retirement of Ellen Waller from the headship of The Mount School approached, the General Committee of the school's governing body met in the autumn of 1938 to consider their options. The outcome of their deliberations and Connie's thoughtful response to them were to prove pivotal in the history of the school and in the life of one of the more visionary teachers of the times.

---

64. SAUL, ECN to DR, January 6, 1931, ms38515/5/96/2. The Council is the "supreme governing body of the University" responsible for its strategic outlook, its financial well-being, and administrative competence. The university's other major deliberative body is the Court, which provides opportunity for public discussion of all aspects of the university.
65. SAUL, ECN to DR, January 4, 1934, ms38515/5/96/3.

CHAPTER

6

THE MOUNT SCHOOL, YORK

George Fox, the most prominent amongst the leaders of the religious movement known as the Society of Friends (the Quakers), arrived in York two days before Christmas 1651. There, according to his autobiography, he encountered "severall [sic] people that was very tender." By this he meant a group of people well-disposed to Quaker ideas, dissenters from the established church who could be counted "seekers" after truth. These men and women represent the beginnings of the Quaker movement in York. In spite of harassment from the established churches – George Fox himself was thrown down the steps of York Minster – the group survived and flourished.[1]

Towards the end of the eighteenth century two members of this group, Esther and William Tuke, made noteworthy gifts to the city. Exemplifying the Quaker spirit of consideration for others, the Quaker belief that Christ is in every human being, and a commitment to the benefits of education and health, in 1785 Esther (1727–94) founded a school for Quaker girls on Trinity Lane,[2] and ten years later her husband, William (1732–1822), appalled by the treatment of a Quaker widow in the York lunatic asylum, built The Retreat, a spacious new hospital for the mentally disturbed where more humane methods of treatment were to be used.

Esther Tuke's school on Trinity Lane moved to a larger site on Tower Street, closer to the Friends' Meeting House and the Tukes' residence but

---

1. David Alexander Scott, "Politics, Dissent and Quakerism in York, 1640–1700" (Ph.D. diss., Dept. History, University of York, 1990).
2. Alfred James Peacock, *Essays in York History* (York: York Settlement Trust, 1997).

fell on hard times. Closed in 1814 for lack of funds, it nevertheless had begun the tradition of the education of Quaker girls in the city. In 1831 another Quaker girls' school, supervised by Samuel Tuke, grandson of Esther and William, opened its doors in Castlegate. Twenty-five years later it too moved to a more open location outside the city on Dalton Terrace in an area known as The Mount. These two schools together shaped the founding principles and ongoing aspirations of today's Mount School [Fig. 6.1].[3]

The Appointment of a New Headmistress

On October 14, 1938, the General Committee of the governing body of the school took up the question of the search for a new Headmistress. The retirement of Ellen C. Waller, who had led the school with great distinction for over a decade, was to take place at the end of the academic year. A subcommittee comprising Lettice Jowitt, Margaret Harvey, Mary Rowntree, Henry Fryer, Christine Ellis, Marion Wilkinson, and Arnold Rowntree was charged with soliciting applications and making recommendations. It was hoped that a short list could be in hand for the January 1939 meeting.[4]

At the January 24 meeting Dr. Fryer reported that a short list had been drawn up and the top three candidates, Mary Stewart, Helen Loge, and Mary Jewell, had been interviewed. None, however, was thought by the subcommittee to be exactly qualified for the post. Faced with this report, the full committee, aware of Connie Nightingale's excellent record as a teacher at The Mount for four years already (1920–4) and of her reputation as an energetic, outward-looking, and visionary Head of Dr. Williams' School, agreed unanimously that the headship be offered to her. The fact that she was a Quaker will not have been a disadvantage. Further consideration should be deferred, they agreed, until they heard back from Miss Nightingale.[5]

Some idea of the soul-searching with which Connie considered this offer may be gleaned from letters written to her by Aladin, but nothing ex-

---

3. For an engaging account of the history of the school, see Sarah Sheils, *Among Friends: The Story of The Mount School, York* (London: James & James, 2007).
4. BIY, Minute Book 1927–39, MOU 1/2/1/6, General Committee 14/10/1938.
5. BIY, Minute Book 1927–39, MOU 1/2/1/6, General Committee 24/1/1939.

Fig. 6.1. *School House, The Mount School, York, 2020.*
(Photo: Courtesy The Mount School, York)

presses better both her reluctance to leave Wales and her heartfelt commitment to a future at and for The Mount than the letter she wrote to the governors:

> My sense of duty to and deep affection for those for whom I work seemed at first an insuperable obstacle to my giving you the answer that you and the committee desired. But it gradually became clear that I must be willing to put myself at the disposal of your committee as a channel of service to The Mount and the Society of Friends.[6]

At the time (early 1939), however, Connie was deeply involved at Dr. Williams' School not only with curricula and staff decisions but also with extensive construction projects. She herself had taken a hand in the architectural plans for a new hall and library, and in engaging Edward Barnsley to design and make the furniture for them. Barnsley's workshop had also been contracted to refurbish the Dining Hall and the dormitories.

---

6. Cited from Muriel Putz in her obituary: "E. Constance Nightingale," *The Friend* (January 5, 1968), p. 10.

Since these projects would not be finished until the summer, and follow-up work would need to be dealt with, she could not see her way clear to leave Dolgellau until the following spring.

On the 21st of February, the chair reported to the full committee on the talks with Miss Nightingale, the conclusion being that she was willing to accept their invitation but could not take up the appointment at The Mount until Easter 1940. Discussions about salary were ongoing, but Miss Waller had agreed to continue in the headship until Miss Nightingale arrived, and both had agreed to consider together what improvements should be made to the Headmistress's house.[7] On this basis, things moved forward.

At a meeting of the General Committee on May 26, with all details decided, a warm welcome was extended to Miss Nightingale in her presence and great "thankfulness expressed that she had felt it right to accept the post of Headmistress."[8] Almost a year was to pass before she took up her appointment, in the course of which war broke out between Britain and Germany.

During the 1930s fearful events had shaken the world. International agreements in Europe were broken by Adolf Hitler's unswerving ambition to extend German *Lebensraum* by attaching first Austria (1938), then Czechoslovakia (1938–9) and Poland (1939) to Germany. The imminence of the threat from Nazi Germany was brought home to the girls at The Mount by the presence amongst them of Jewish refugees spirited out of Germany by the *Kindertransport* scheme. Supported by refugee aid committees, including the Quakers, this scheme brought Jewish children in late 1938 and early 1939 to England, where their well-being – a home, health, clothing, education, and holidays – was guaranteed.[9] Following the German invasion of Poland, in accordance with their treaty obligations, Britain and France declared war on Germany on September 3, 1939. For the first six months or so of the war, the time immediately preceding Connie's move

---

7. BIY, Minute Book 1927–39, MOU 1/2/1/6, Subcommittee 21/2/1939.
8. BIY, Minute Book 1927–39, MOU 1/2/1/6, General Committee 26/5/1939.
9. Connie Nightingale's brother, Tom, and his wife, Marion, sponsored one of these Jewish girls, Marta Kurc, who lived with them throughout the war, at the end of which she immigrated to Canada, becoming an influential journalist and editor in Toronto.

to York, there was so little engagement between the opposing forces that the period became known as the "Phoney War." In North Wales things were quiet, and Dr. Williams' School went about its business in a relatively normal manner, enabling Connie to tie up loose ends and prepare for the move to York. She continued her correspondence with David Russell, at year's end optimistically expressing the wish, "May all of us have the joy of seeing ourselves building a better world."[10]

Many of the larger towns and cities in Britain, however, in anticipation of German air raids, were planning their defences, positioning anti-aircraft guns and barrage balloons, building air-raid shelters, and distributing gas masks. The safety of children was paramount, and plans were made for many to be evacuated to the countryside or more remote parts of England, and even to Canada. York was no exception to these nationwide concerns. Amidst scenes of feverish activity, houses in the town, including one of the larger of The Mount School's buildings, were commandeered by the military, while the railway station witnessed the movement of large quantities of war materials and unusual numbers of passengers. It was obvious that the station, an important transport and communications link, would sooner or later be a target for German bombers. The vulnerable position of The Mount School, close to the railway line and the station's marshalling yards, gave the school's governors cause for alarm, so their decision to move the girls out of harm's way came as no surprise. For the start of the autumn term the school moved, lock, stock, and barrel, to a large country house, Cober Hill, on the Yorkshire coast.

Cober Hill had been set up shortly after World War I as a summer guest house and conference centre for the use mainly of the York Adult School.[11] As such it was not ideally suited for use as a boarding school, especially in the winter months, but it had the advantages of size and availability. At short notice the domestic staff, the housekeeper, and a handful of teachers and senior girls rearranged the rooms as classrooms, studies, bedrooms, and dormitories; with the conversion of the conservatory into a laboratory and other ingenious solutions to teaching needs, Cober Hill offered the

10. SAUL, ECN to DR, December 30, 1939, ms38515/5/96/3.
11. The Adult School in York was inaugurated and supported by local Quakers, amongst whom the Rowntree family was prominent.

necessary spaces for the two terms the girls were to be in residence. Eighty-seven girls arrived at the beginning of the autumn term, understandably fewer than the 119 of the 1938–9 school year, and gamely put up with the hardships of dislocation, the cold weather, and uncertainty about the future. During these winter months the governors took steps to ensure that in York the wartime blackout rules (whereby all windows and doors were covered at night) could be followed, and an underground air-raid shelter (of a sort) was prepared. As it was, York suffered no air raids while the girls were at Cober Hill, and staff and students were able to return to their address at The Mount just before Easter 1940. They were in time to welcome Connie Nightingale to the headship.

1940–1942

The initial impact of the war had been met by the removal of the school to Cober Hill and the initiation of air-raid precautions at The Mount; yet there was much for Connie to ponder as she took up her new responsibilities [Fig. 6.2]. At Dr. Williams' School she had concentrated on boosting the numbers of pupils and staff; on the construction or acquisition of new buildings and land; on building a broader curriculum with emphasis on music; on international awareness; on academic success; and on paying attention to advantages the region had to offer – the Welsh language, Welsh culture and customs, and the glorious countryside. Similar themes were at the front of her mind in York. But to these in wartime York were added other concerns: unexpected financial worries, the rationing of food, petrol rationing, clothing coupons, and other restrictions. Perhaps most troubling to Connie, though less immediate, were the changes in education an unpredictable postwar climate might bring.

Unforeseen financial obligations, such as the provision of admittedly rudimentary air-raid shelters, could not be covered by the school's budget and had to be met by volunteer contributions. Alumnae, parents, and friends, amongst whom Quaker families played a leading role, generously chipped in. Petrol rationing restricted everyone's movements: sporting fixtures with more distant schools were discontinued, compensated for by games with other groups and schools in York itself, and intensified study of the city's

Fig. 6.2. *Connie Nightingale as Headmistress of The Mount School, York, 1940–8, portrait head. (Artist: Richard Naish. Photo: Courtesy The Mount School, York)*

cultural riches took the place of cultural visits further afield. Parents' visits were limited, and staff too felt this hardship. Food rationing presented urgent problems, and though the catering staff did their best, the absence of meat and butter was sorely felt. Margarine was no substitute for butter, and whale meat or horse meat in place of beef, pork, lamb, or chicken was not greeted favourably – though the appearance of bowls of dripping and bread at teatime was welcome.

The girls were kept up to date with news of the war (though some complained that not enough information was given), including the activities of the British army in France, the retreat to Dunkirk, and the chaotic but heroic withdrawal across the channel. Many girls contributed to the war effort, some by knitting socks, blankets, and gloves for the troops; others interested in first aid turned to nursing and linked up with the St. John's Ambulance brigade. Still others worked in the school's gardens: new vegetable patches were opened with the help of boys from Bootham School, some girls becoming enthusiastic enough to go to work in the summer holidays as "land girls," in effect replacing young farm workers who had gone off to war.[12]

Despite the setbacks the army had suffered, and the retreat from France, morale amongst the girls was high, sustained by the victory of the RAF in the Battle of Britain (July–October 1940). Enrollment figures improved in 1941, and the school, parents, and alumnae came together in March 1941 to celebrate the 110th anniversary of the foundation. The occasion was the more festive for the presence of Bootham boys,[13] who came up from town for the events, and for the announcement of the establishment of a School Birthday Bursary Fund set up by generous donors. Connie's knowledge of contemporary world affairs, however, her connections in London political and cultural circles, and her personal experience of European geography and ways of doing business prompted her to sound a note of caution. Aware of the need for, and the inevitability of, social change in Britain – including wide-ranging changes in education both public and private – in her report to the Board of Governors she warned of changes in the wind for which the schools must be ready. The governors must be resolute, she said, in promoting confidence amongst students, staff, and parents and in their commitment to the promotion of Christian values in the schools.

Connie's continued correspondence with David Russell – her first letter from The Mount is dated July 2, 1940 – reveals the fullness of her awareness of the political situation in which the independent schools found themselves, and of the state of the war. As to the war, they agreed that Ireland, Spain, and the French navy presented the most immediate problems, and that control of the air was critical.[14] Many of their letters however concerned Alexis Aladin's future (he would be seventeen on December 23) [Fig. 6.3], Connie wondering whether a career in engineering or medicine

---

12. Women who volunteered to work on farms year-round became known as the "Women's Land Army."
13. This was an early instance of Connie's encouragement of interaction between young women and young men, aimed at prompting social ease.
14. SAUL, DR to ECN, July 3, 1940, ms38515/5/96/3.

Fig. 6.3. *Alexis Jr. as a teenager. (Photo: Courtesy John Rylands University of Manchester Library, Special Collections)*

would be best for him (Russell's preference was for engineering); and if the war continued, should it be the Royal Navy?[15]

Spring of the following year brought no decision; if anything, the situation was more complicated, with other options under consideration. Should Alexis spend a year studying Russian at the London School of Slavonic and East European Studies, now housed in Oxford, where admission would be straightforward,[16] or should he stay another year at Bootham? If called up, was the Fleet Air Arm the place for him? He was very keen on flying. If he wished to pursue engineering should he train as an apprentice or would a university degree be better?[17] A month later, when Alexis announced he was not keen on Russian studies, Russell was emphatic. He

---

15. SAUL, ECN to DR, July 2, 1940, ms38515/96/3.
16. A friend of Connie's, Mary Braunholtz, whose husband was Professor of Comparative Philology at Oxford, had written as much.
17. SAUL, ECN to DR, March 10, 1941, ms38515/96/3.

should not do Russian; work in an engineering shop or in business would be a better preparation for university. Russell's brother-in-law, a civil engineer, strongly advised that Alexis take a B.Sc. in engineering, suggesting Cambridge or Edinburgh, whereas Russell himself put in a word for St. Andrews.[18] Though Bootham wanted Alexis to stay on for a further year as Head of School, he himself was against it, and Connie agreed. Russell tried throughout July to get him admitted to Edinburgh, and he visited and was interviewed, all to no avail; by October Connie was ready to leave any decision about his future to Russell.[19]

Russell's response to Connie's appeal was to invoke the help of a professional tutor in Edinburgh, Basil Paterson.[20] After spending a weekend with the Russell family at their home in Fife, Alexis consulted Paterson,[21] who proved to be as expert in negotiating the intricacies of entrance to English and Scottish universities as he was in teaching subject matter. In Edinburgh Paterson set him to work at once, writing at length to Connie explaining how Alexis's strengths and weaknesses could best be used to get him into the university of his choice. Paterson's knowledge and experience went a long way towards sorting out the difficulties in which Connie and Alexis found themselves,[22] mapping out a route for him to begin Engineering studies at Edinburgh in October 1942. The following month Connie mentioned to David Russell how satisfied Alexis was with life in Edinburgh, and reiterated her thanks for his taking the lead in arranging the next steps in Alexis's education. At the same time, she urged that some practical work be found for him in the summer.

When sometime in mid-December Paterson heard of a new four-term course at Cambridge University planned specially for students prior to their call up for military service he asked Connie whether he should put in an application on Alexis's behalf.[23] He had written to Pembroke College at Cambridge outlining Alexis's situation. The Tutor at Pembroke, J. W. F.

---

18. SAUL, DR to ECN, April 15 and 17, 1941, ms38515/96/3.
19. SAUL, ECN to DR, October 2, 1941.
20. Of Paterson and Ainslie, Tutors, 17 Palmerston Place, Edinburgh.
21. SAUL, DR to ECN, October 6, 1941, ms38515/5/96/3.
22. SAUL, BP to ECN, October 14, 1941, ms38515/5/96/3.
23. SAUL, ECN to DR, December 29, 1941, ms38515/96/3.

Rowe, said he would consider Alexis's admission in May or October, subject to his coming to Cambridge for interviews and his passing the Latin Previous and Mechanical Sciences Qualifying exams in March. He added that the university could not consider his admission to the Mechanical Sciences Tripos until October.[24] Alexis's enthusiasm for airplanes and flying, however, was undiminished; he was eager to volunteer for the Fleet Air Arm, telling Connie that "there was a long waiting list, and he would have no chance unless he volunteered early in the New Year."[25]

On January 20 Alexis travelled to Pembroke for interviews with Rowe and the Director of Studies in Mechanical Sciences, returning north from Cambridge to Edinburgh via York the following day. In York he relayed to Connie a message from the Tutor asking for a letter of recommendation for him from David Russell; whereupon Connie wrote to Russell with the request.[26] Three days later Rowe wrote to Connie of the college's conditional acceptance of Alexis for the Easter term, following up with a letter to Russell confirming the college's decision.[27] Alexis's life as a Cambridge undergraduate was about to begin. That he was in residence for four terms (Easter and Michaelmas terms 1942, and Lent and Easter 1943) is confirmed by the college's archives, which also show that he took a Certificate in Proficiency in Engineering Study (Class 2) in October 1942, making clear his intention to proceed to the Mechanical Sciences Tripos after the war. That he took an active part in the social and sporting life of the college is shown by his membership in the College Boat Club, his presence in the 1st May Boat, and the award of his college colors.[28]

At York, the girls of The Mount School had taken wartime conditions in their stride, not allowing all the changes involved to interfere too much with their daily rounds. In fact, they took to their studies with such interest and purpose that the results of public examinations in 1942 were excellent. No fewer than five of the twenty-plus girls who successfully passed

---

24. SAUL, JWFR to BP, December 22, 1941, ms38515/5/96/3.
25. Volunteering did not mean being called up at once; it often involved long delays.
26. SAUL, ECN to DR, January 21, 1942, ms38515/5/96/3.
27. SAUL, JWFR to DR, February 2, 1942, ms38515/5/96/3.
28. Email communication from E. Ennion-Smith, Archivist, Pembroke College, Cambridge University, July 5, 2019.

the Higher School Certificate exams went on to Oxford University, while others were admitted to London University or Sheffield, one amongst them a scholarship winner in science. Others began professional careers, through training courses or apprenticeships in medicine, pharmacy, nursing, and other caring professions. In these successes it is easy to see the hand of Connie Nightingale; her unruffled insistence on the importance of more opportunity for women in life and on the value of public service guided many girls towards a life of learning and a professional career. This focus on the significance of learning and its practical applications, especially for young women, as promulgated at The Mount, led to an increasing popularity of the school amongst parents. It supported the governors' decisions to admit more pupils, lower the age of admission, expand the curriculum to include more science, hire more teachers, and acquire more space.

These decisions, advanced and supported by Connie, anticipated the stipulations of the Education Act of 1944.[29] This act sought to iron out contradictions in the governance of education across the country and rectify unfairness in accessibility to secondary education. Administration was to be devolved to local authorities, and secondary education was to be free for every child. There were to be three categories of secondary school: grammar, technical, and modern, the choice of school dependent on the results of the nationwide so-called 11+ exam (taken at age 11+) and teachers' reports. The impact on private schools of the state's commitment to secondary education was obvious and widely debated; it was a topic paid serious attention by the Governors of The Mount, and knowledge of its intentions contributed forcefully to their decision to expand the school's physical presence, as well as the number and diversity of students and staff. They were fortunate that Connie – given her work for and contacts at the Board of Education – was fully aware of the developments leading up to the act.

---

29. Building on the 1938 Spens Report submitted by a committee chaired by Sir Will Spens, Master of Corpus Christi College, Cambridge, and on a 1941 Board of Education internal memorandum, *Education after the War*, the Education Act of 1944 was guided through Parliament by the President of the Board of Education, R. A. Butler (hence the "Butler Act").

A firm believer in the benefits to be derived from the study of music and the arts, Connie moved to expand the scope and quality of instruction in these areas; in this she followed the path she had pursued with great success at Dr. Williams' School. What's more, her continuing belief in international responsibility, as exemplified by her membership (and we may recall, that of Dr. Williams' School) in the League of Nations (1920–46), is underscored by the addition of European refugees to the staff. And her belief in political morality is made plain by the appearance of conscientious objectors also on the staff. Amongst these was Edward Barnsley, who gave a great boost and new meaning to the teaching of art: he gave classes both in basic carpentry and in other aspects of woodwork – in design, in decoration, in the qualities and uses of materials, and in traditional methods.

At Dr. Williams' School the governors through Connie's agency had hired Barnsley's workshop, a leading group in the Arts and Crafts movement, to do extensive work in a new hall and library complex, in the renovation of the dining hall, and in updating the furniture in the dormitories. The innovations introduced by Barnsley's workshop had induced the girls to think more creatively about refinements in art and had been warmly greeted. At The Mount Barnsley's teaching similarly showed the girls new ways of looking at art and the practical skills by which artistic effects could be created.[30] The purpose of education at The Mount, as Connie explained towards the end of 1942, was to train the girls to be better citizens, to make them alert to the benefits of lifelong learning, to teach them the value of work as a satisfying experience, a realisation of self-worth, and to show them the damaging effects of unemployment. They should be brought, she said, to see the good in every person they met whatever their color, creed, gender, or nationality, and to be able to live and work constructively in any conditions.

In the spring of 1942, the German air force had attacked York. The railway station and its dependencies, their main target, were effectively obliterated. Bombs, randomly released, had also fallen all over the city; important

---

30. Edward Barnsley, whose father and uncle applied new ideas to the design and manufacture of furniture and had moved in 1893 to the Cotswolds to establish their workshop, was known to Connie through her friendship with the Gimsons during her undergraduate days; see Chapter 2.

buildings and private houses were destroyed, many people were killed, and many others wounded. Widespread destruction included property only a few hundred yards from The Mount, but the school itself was spared. As it was, no girls were in residence – it was the Easter holidays – but it was quite a scare. This episode was a sharp reminder of how close danger could come.

1943–1945

Under Connie's thoughtful leadership, and that of the Board of Governors, the school had adjusted well to the dangers and shortages of the first years of the war. The news of the Allies' military victory at El Alamein in the Egyptian desert (October–November 1942), coupled with the successful Russian defence of and victory at Stalingrad (August 1942–January 1943), inspired an optimism that allowed the governors to implement some of the plans outlined during the previous year. The number of students was increased by lowering the age of admission to 11 and, thanks to the improved financial situation of the school, by adding more scholarships. Buildings were bought – including one large house adjacent to the main school buildings – to accommodate these newcomers and provide additional classroom space. More teachers were hired, including scientists, for whom a laboratory and its essential equipment was provided. Outreach efforts, so typical of Connie Nightingale's thinking, included joint performances by the choirs of the two Quaker schools, The Mount and Bootham. This linkage between the two schools, with its implications for every aspect of relations between young women and young men, was increasingly emphasised as the years went by.

An important source for information on this topic is the *Mount Magazine*. The school events calendar for 1943–4 mentions both schools' participation in a Whitsuntide dance, joint exhibitions of art and crafts, and tennis matches involving the staff of both schools as well as students. The Debating Societies met together to discuss propositions such as "the desirability of a state medical service," a motion that lost. Another, proposing that "the place of women is in the house" was notable for the alarm it provoked amongst the Bootham contingent at the prospect of men having to do housework; the motion was defeated by a narrow margin.[31]

The magazine reports the activities of other societies at The Mount too: the Scientific Society, the Geographical Society, the Dramatic Society, the Literary Society, and others, witnessing the breadth of extracurricular activities the girls could enjoy. It published student poems and stories, some illustrated, included student crosswords, puzzles, and competitions, and brought news of weekend activities (e.g., parents' weekend, social services weekend), half holidays, movies, and visiting lecturers. It drew attention to outings to important buildings in York, to concerts, to excursions further afield (e.g., to Rievaulx, where members of the Geographical Society drew plans of the abbey ruins), and to outside escapades such as the shenanigans associated with Halloween. It described manual work done by the girls growing and digging potatoes. With the help of Bootham boys they had dug over the hockey field and turned it into a vegetable patch – a visible contribution to the national "Dig for Victory" campaign. The good health and reputation of both Quaker schools is reflected in the annual report of the chairman of the Board of Governors: demand for places in both schools was rising to the point that both were full for 1945 and almost full for 1946.[32]

Another example of the school's commitment both to the war effort and to community service is the cleanup work at Cober Hill. Following the school's return to York, the house had been commandeered by the army. Soldiers are not best known for domestic tidiness or respect for others' belongings, and their conduct on this occasion was no exception. This respected country house had suffered considerable damage, and the place had been left a mess. Deciding to put things right both in the garden and the house, a party of senior girls set out for the coast, some equipped with hoes and rakes to fettle the gardens and the driveway, others with brushes and dusters to deal with the chaos in the house itself. They were under the eagle eye of Connie's friend Melita Alexander, for a time secretary of

---

31. BIY *Mount Magazine* 1943–4 MOU 6/5/1/55.
32. BIY Annual School Report 1944 MOU/1/4/1/48.

the school. The tidying and cleaning of the house took a week; the drive leading to the house was cleared of fallen tree limbs, overgrowth, and rubbish, and a start made on bringing the gardens into shape.

On the personal side, Connie's correspondence with David Russell continued. They exchanged views on possible speakers at The Mount School (Rev. George MacLeod? Sir Bernard Pares?), the possibility of agreement between the "Anglo-Saxon world" and the USSR, and the candidates to be the next Archbishop of Canterbury (with many misgivings about religious leadership in the UK). Much of their thinking, however, focused on Alexis's whereabouts and his future. In a routine letter to Miss Bell, David Russell's office manager who took care of the quarterly payments Russell made towards Alexis's upkeep, Connie recalls her help with Alexis when he was much younger and mentions that at Cambridge (where he had matriculated on May 4, 1942) he was "longing for a glimpse of the hills after the plains," a liking that echoed his father's delight in the "everlasting hills."[33]

Writing to Russell in the New Year she expressed her hope that he thought Alexis "had been worth educating" and "is developing along the lines you wish," adding that he was "now reconciled to this year in Cambridge although he is aching to fly."[34] It becomes clear from letters later in the year that he volunteered for the Fleet Air Arm perhaps as early as January 1942 and was called up in summer 1943 after finishing his Cambridge pre-call-up course. After initial training at the Royal Naval Air Station Crail (HMS Jackdaw) in Scotland, he was posted to Canada for flight training under the British Commonwealth Air Training Plan. Connie and the Russell family were able to exchange letters with him, but Connie was unable despite all her efforts to send money.[35] Back in Scotland by early summer 1944 Alexis spent some time with the Russell family on Iona, and later in the summer visited them at their flat in Eglinton Crescent, Edinburgh: he seemed happy and looked well.[36] In September he phoned Connie telling her he was to be stationed north of Inverness, presumably at HMS Field-

---

33. SAUL, ECN to JB, August 12 ,1942, ms3515/5/96/3.
34. SAUL, ECN to DR, January 15, 1943, ms3515/5/96/3.
35. ECN to DR, November 25 and December 24, 1943, ms3515/5/96/3.
36. SAUL, DR to ECN, July 14 and August 22, 1944, ms3515/5/96/4.

fare, an airfield on the shore of Cromarty Firth.[37] His life came to a sudden and utterly unexpected end on January 3, 1945. Listed formally as "missing, presumed killed," Sub-Lieutenant Alexis Aladin, RNVR (Royal Naval Volunteer Reserve), died on active service a few weeks after his twenty-first birthday. Connie was devastated.[38]

David and Alison Russell suffered grievous loss too. Of their two sons, the younger, Captain Patrick Russell, Royal Artillery, served in Egypt in 1943, and, attached to the London Scottish regiment, in Italy. He died of wounds on September 7, 1944. The elder, Captain David F. O. Russell of the 7th Battalion, Black Watch, was seriously wounded at El Alamein, where he was awarded the Military Cross. He was wounded again in Sicily. Promoted Major and second-in-command of his battalion, he landed in Normandy on D-Day plus four, only to be seriously wounded yet again at Le Havre.[39] He survived and was invalided out. In later life he became a successful, community-minded businessman, a university administrator, a philanthropist, and fervent supporter of the National Trust for Scotland.

1945–1948

The war ended in Europe on May 8, 1945, and with Japan on August 14. Amid scenes of general jubilation, The Mount School enjoyed a two days' holiday. Girls who lived nearby went home to be with their families; others were allowed out of school to wander about York. The return to routine schoolwork put a damper on all the excitement, however, and normal conditions resumed quickly. Civics Week was held as usual, the theme this year being "Women and Their Work," one day focusing on women famous in the worlds of art, literature, medicine, or politics, another day on the current work of old girls of the school. Some were working for the Friends

---

37. SAUL, ECN to DR, September 10, 1944, ms3515/5/96/4.
38. Alexis's name appears on the stone war memorial in Dolgellau, on the Roll of Honour Board at Bootham School, on the Memorial Plaque in the Cloisters of Pembroke College, Cambridge, and on the Lee-on-Solent Fleet Air Arm Memorial.
39. The War Office telegrams informing the Russells of the death of their younger son in Italy and the serious wounding of the elder in France were delivered, by hideous coincidence, on the same day: Lorn Macintyre, *Sir David Russell: A Biography* (Edinburgh: Canongate, 1994), p. 212.

Relief Service helping refugees in the Middle East or children hospitalised in Mauritius, others continuing their work in the WRNS (Women's Royal Naval Service) and similar governmental activities.

Though the war was won, the country was on the verge of bankruptcy, and there was no sign of a break with the austerity of the war years. Shortages and rationing continued. The shortage of fuel was felt most acutely in the absence of hot water and heat. Dormitories were cold, hot-water bottles could be filled only from a water heater in the basement, and the girls were allowed only two baths a week. The extreme cold of the winter of 1947 did not help matters. Food and clothing were still rationed, the limited supply of food an all too palpable hardship.

The rationing of food, implemented by the issue of ration books, had been introduced early in 1940. Butter, sugar, and bacon were the first items to be rationed, though all other basic foods – except for bread and potatoes – were soon restricted. There were obvious loopholes: those living in the countryside or in contact with farmers could sometimes come home with an extra egg or two, or even a side of ham, and this level of black market was widely tolerated. The end of the war did not alter these conditions, so food at The Mount continued to be all too monotonous.[40] Though the meals themselves were unappetising, they did remind the girls that theirs was a Quaker school. Another reminder that The Mount was a Quaker foundation was the underscoring of the belief in the value of silence, a belief acknowledged as the girls filed quietly into the dining room, and by the period of silence held, as a form of "grace," before meals began.

Clothes rationing (1941–9), applicable to everyone (with exceptions for children and special groups, e.g., those needing uniforms) was mitigated by programmes such as the self-explanatory "Make Do and Mend" effort. The limited supply of clothes was not felt by the Mount girls as sharply as the rationing of food, but all the same it made extra demands on their capacity for self-help and ingenuity.[41]

Connie's correspondence with David Russell continued during this period, but to judge by the evidence of the St. Andrews archives, much less

---

40. Food rationing did not end completely until 1954, nine years after the end of the war, when meat and bacon were the last commodities to be freed.
41. Sheils, 97–9.

frequently. In October 1944 Connie had written after the death of David's younger son in Italy and the wounding of the other in France, offering her and Alexis's condolences: "Alexis's heart is very sad, as is mine, at the thought of all your suffering and his own inability to ease the burden," concluding, "your heartache must be great. I trust that strength will be given you."[42] She cannot possibly have imagined at that moment that within three months the war would have taken Alexis too. The summoning of courage and equanimity to resume her duties at The Mount School almost immediately is testament to her remarkable spiritual strength.

No letters from 1945 between the two seem to have survived. However, when the 1946 New Year's Honours List announced a knighthood for David Russell, the correspondence resumed, Connie enthusiastically acknowledging the award in a letter of January 7:

> My dear David,
> This brings warmest congratulations on your well-deserved honour. A Scottish friend has just been here for lunch, and if the world rewarded as deserved you would have to be canonized not knighted, for as someone speaking to her in Peebles said, "You see Dr. Russell is a saint and he runs his works in that same spirit." Of all the people I know Aladin senior would have rejoiced more than anyone at this honour "to my David" as he called you.[43]

Her mention of Aladin leads to comments on the "mystery of life after death, psychic phenomena, and the Quest Society,"[44] areas of thought which Aladin had probed repeatedly. She ends with regrets that she can't help Anne (Russell's youngest daughter) and with intimations that she isn't as strong or as engaged as she used to be: "I feel so pressed for time that I do not seem to get down to much outside the daily round. I long to help but am stale."[45] The school's wartime difficulties and Alexis's death had clearly taken a heavy toll.

---

42. SAUL, ECN to DR, undated October 1944, ms38515/96/4.
43. SAUL, ECN to DR, January 7, 1946, ms38515/5/96/4.
44. Founded by G. R. S. Mead (1863–1933) as a branch of the Theosophical Society, the Quest Society sought spiritual knowledge in studying science and philosophy, comparing religious experience, and investigating extrasensory perception. The Society published a periodical, *The Quest*.
45. SAUL, ECN to DR, January 7, 1946, ms38515/5/96/4.

She was in brighter mood when she wrote in March. In Aberystwyth for a meeting of the Council of the University of Wales, on which she had served since 1931, she had talked on several occasions with the President of the University, Thomas Jones. Jones, an old acquaintance with a long-standing interest in education and the founder in 1927 of Coleg Harlech (adult education) not far (about twelve miles) from Dr. Williams' School, had been a high-ranking British civil servant[46] and was Chair of the Pilgrim Trust.[47] Connie took up with him the question of the publication of some of Aladin's letters which Jones agreed should be published, preferably with a foreword by Russell. She added in her letter[48] that she had in mind a trip to America where she could approach Raphael Zon to contribute to a foreword for an American edition.[49] While in Aberystwyth she had also set up at the university a Scholarship Fund, to be called the Alexis Aladin Travel Scholarship, to be used for lecturers or honour students for travel in Russia. Some of her old vim and vigor had returned.

In June Russell wrote to Connie agreeing to support the application of two Mount girls to St. Andrews University, and again, later in the year,[50] on an unidentified problem troubling Connie that seemed difficult to him too:

> I have been carrying about with me the correspondence I had with you during the summer, along with the letters you sent me, always hoping to be able to make some definite suggestions which might be helpful. It is difficult to know just what to do, and I feel the only satisfactory way to make progress would be to have a talk over the whole matter.

---

46. After serving in various academic and governmental positions, Jones (1870–1955) moved to the Cabinet Secretariat in London. There between 1916 and 1930 he served as Deputy Secretary to the Cabinet under four Prime Ministers, amongst them Lloyd George and Stanley Baldwin.
47. Founded in 1930 by an American, Edward Harkness, the Pilgrim Trust made grants to charities and individuals for the preservation of historically significant buildings or documents.
48. SAUL, ECN to DR, March 1, 1946, ms38515/5/96/4.
49. Zon, a contemporary of Aladin's at school in Simbirsk and at Kazan University, is mentioned (as Rafael) in Aladin's letters, and like him had been a fugitive from Russia in the late 1890s. In America Zon became Professor of Forestry at the University of Minnesota.
50. SAUL, DR to ECN, June 26, 1946, ms38515/5/96/4, and October 17, 1946, ms38515/96/4.

He went on to say that he hopes she can visit them in Scotland during the Christmas holidays when they could "talk over everything and arrange how to proceed." By early December, however, Connie is planning to go to Constantinople (referred to as such in the letters, though the name of the city had been changed to Istanbul in 1930) to meet Russell's daughter Anne. However, a visit to Silverburn, the Russells' home in Fife, is also on her calendar.[51] What was this problem vexing Connie that Russell too was finding intractable?

Only brief letters survive from 1947, two from Russell to Connie and one from her to him. One of his asked whether she could meet them in London,[52] the other included a letter he had received from Professor John Macmurray.[53] Replying hurriedly, she says she cannot get to London – it would mean changing too many appointments – but she had read the Macmurray letter and would reply to it later. Her handwriting, already deteriorating in 1946, is untidier and more irregular; and there are insertions, last-minute additions perhaps. The tone is almost of exasperation, quite different from the tone of her letters before Alexis's death. She sounds tired.[54] Since this brief correspondence centres on Professor Macmurray, an eminent Scottish philosopher and student of reason and emotion, could it be that his thoughts had some bearing on the problem troubling her six months previously? Or was the worry about the state of her health, physical and mental? And what impact might such considerations have on the timing of her retirement from the headship?

Her health had always been less than robust, and she had frequently remarked on it to Russell, his replies often advocating unconventional remedies which had helped him in his youth and in which he continued to believe.[55] Given her comments about "being stale," her fatigue, her lack

---

51. SAUL, DR to ECN, December 13, 1946, ms38515/5/96/4.
52. SAUL, DR to ECN, May 1, 1947, ms38515/5/96/4.
53. SAUL, DR to ECN, May 6, 1947, ms38515/5/96/4. John Macmurray was Professor of Moral Philosophy at the University of Edinburgh (1944–58), previously Professor of Mind and Logic at University College London (1928–44) and Fellow and Tutor at Balliol College, Oxford (1922–8).
54. SAUL, ECN to DR, undated May 1947, ms38515/5/96/4.
55. Russell had been helped by the recommendations of the Kellgren Institute: physiotherapy, fresh air, exercise, and organic food; see Macintyre, pp. 10 ff.

Fig. 6.4. *Connie Nightingale with Kathleen Carrick Smith, the new Headmistress of The Mount, in 1948. (Photo: From R. F. Christian,* Alexis Aladin: The Tragedy of Exile, *p. 153, fig. 26)*

of energy and not having enough time, was she thinking of retirement, and had she already in autumn 1946 been contemplating it? To judge from the circumstances before her own appointment to the headship, the governors liked a year to interview candidates. If Connie had been thinking of retiring at the end of the school year 1947–8, her thoughts would have been discussed with the governors during academic 1946–7, the very time at which she had asked Russell for advice. When her retirement, at the age of 55, took place in September 1948 [Fig. 6.4], it was on the grounds of ill health, a circumstance confirmed by the first letter surviving from 1948 between her and Russell.

Writing from her cottage in Wales a couple of months after leaving The Mount, she is busy settling into a new life in familiar surroundings and coping with her aches and pains. Her doctor thinks she has "arthritis in the head," which she says is painful; but she is to see an orthopedic specialist "on Saturday" who "has not seen me nor the X ray plates yet."[56] She asks Russell if he has a cure, evidently hoping that alternative medicines might offer a remedy. Otherwise, she comments briefly on the memorials for Alexis, and on the publication of his father's letters and papers.[57] Her health is uppermost in her mind, and anxiety about it surely played a large part in her decision to retire.

---

56. SAUL, ECN to DR, undated November 1948, ms36515/5/96/4.
57. Finally published as "A Childhood" in the *Rothmill Quarterly* 26 (1954–5) and 27 (1955–6). For more on the *Rothmill Quarterly* see Chapter 7, note 13.

CHAPTER
7

WALES AGAIN: THE RETIREMENT YEARS

The duties and responsibilities of the headship of a school during peacetime are demanding enough; during wartime they multiply in so many ways as to become overwhelming. At her retirement in 1948 Connie's health was giving cause for concern – and she was exhausted. It is easy, then, to imagine both her sense of relief and her disappointment at leaving Yorkshire and returning to her cottage in Wales. Situated on the lower slopes of Cader Idris overlooking Dolgellau, before the war Ty Newydd [Fig. 7.1] had provided a home for her godson Alexis Aladin as he grew up, and for her a place away from the hustle and bustle of school. It was also a home where she could entertain school visitors, and a place of privilege for senior girls. Now she would use the strength and calm of this haven to remedy her ills and pull herself together. Supportive doctors, the tranquillity of the cottage and its setting, the good wishes of colleagues far and wide, the friendship of local people who remembered and admired her, offered spiritual refreshment and a road to better health.

Up to this point in her life three often overlapping areas – education, social problems, and international affairs – had commanded much of her attention.

As a girl at Burnley Grammar School she had first recognised the significance of EDUCATION as a general good and specifically as a means of improving opportunities for young women. At Manchester University her eyes had been opened to the intricacies of language learning, and to the broader horizons of knowledge. She had become acquainted with the suffragette movement in its heartland, and with Quakerism, and had put her principles to work for the University Settlement in Ancoats. Her principal mentors, Ronald Burrows and Phoebe Sheavyn, had showed her the ins and outs of academic life and the value of collegial support. At Lady Manners School and at The Mount School she experienced education from the teacher's desk. Headships at Dr. Williams' School and at the Mount had enabled her to encourage girls' hunger for intellectual stimulation and had involved her in problems of educational policy and leadership.

SOCIAL PROBLEMS had been visible to her from an early age. The difficulties her mother faced when abandoned by her husband had struck home. The poverty she saw in the streets around her, the discrepancies in housing, nourishment, clothing, and cleanliness she witnessed in Burnley as a girl had been amplified by what she saw in Manchester and Leicester as an undergraduate. And she had seen the physical and emotional damage inflicted by World War I. Whereas her brother had survived, this was not the case for many Burnley families: thousands of young men had been killed or wounded. It was painfully obvious that the war had been most severe on the poorer families, revealing social inequities of frightening scale. Furthermore, her interest in national social problems had extended to the international, into uncompromising hatred of war and a firm commitment to peace.

Knowing that a Peace Conference was to take place in Paris in 1919, and determined to support the cause of peace, Connie had looked for a way to participate in INTERNATIONAL AFFAIRS. In these circumstances it seems natural that she should turn to Ronald Burrows, her Professor of Greek at Manchester, for advice, and it is easy to imagine Burrows mentioning Connie to his friends, Greek Prime Minister Eleftherios Venizelos and Konstantinos Spanoudis, a leading member of the London Committee of Unredeemed Greeks. It is surely through the friendship of these two powerful Greeks and the philhellene Burrows that Connie came to be present in Paris. There she served as assistant to the National Committee of Unredeemed Greeks, whose primary concern in Paris was for those Greeks living in Turkey who had recently been expelled from their homes and were now refugees. Two years later when further negotiations with the Turkish government were called for in London, Connie assisted the Greek delega-

Fig. 7.1. *Ty Newydd, Connie Nightingale's house on the lower slopes of Cader Idris, 1930s. (Photo: From programme of Memorial Service held at Dr. Williams' School, Dolgellau, Merioneth, January 31, 1968, p. 18, author's collection)*

tion again. It is worth recalling that for her work in Paris and London the Patriarch of Jerusalem awarded her the Gold Cross of the Holy Sepulchre, a decoration normally reserved for Greeks by birth.

If support for the idea of peace was one of Connie's determined beliefs, helping refugees was another. Her work at the Paris Conference ended, Connie had been asked by Spanoudis to go to Constantinople to help directly with the refugees and to work on his newspaper, *Proodos*.

An extraordinary coincidence was responsible for the expansion of these interests. On a train journey in September 1920 returning from Constantinople to London she met the man she was to be occupied with for the rest of her life – long after the end of his. A Russian politician, leader of the Peasant Party in the dying years of the czarist regime, a spellbinding orator and voracious intellectual, Alexis Aladin had been expelled from Russia on more than one occasion for seditious activity. At the time of his meeting with Connie he was an officer in the White Russian army and an emissary from the White government to Russian émigrés in Paris and London. A long correspondence developed between Aladin and Connie, half of which (from him to her) is archived at Manchester University. Nothing speaks more tellingly of their fondness for one another, though, than her becoming godmother to his son and, after Aladin's death, a surrogate mother to the boy, also named Alexis.

In this way Connie's international interests expanded from Britain and Europe to Russia and its history, culture, politics, and religion. In pursuing these interests Connie was amongst the first to join the London-based Society for Cultural Relations between the Peoples of the British Commonwealth and the Union of Socialist Soviet Republics, known more simply as the SCR. Established in 1924 by a distinguished group of British intellectuals including Bertrand Russell, Virginia Woolf, and Maynard Keynes, the society's purpose was the study of Soviet and British science, art, literature, philosophy, economics, and education. It had been an easy step for her to embrace interests in this wider world.

She had became involved in the League of Nations (founded in 1920), subscribing wholeheartedly to its objectives: to support international co-operation, guarantee peace, settle disputes by negotiation, and deal with refugee problems. As Head of Dr. Williams' School she had enrolled the school, and the girls individually, in the League, confirming her belief in internationalism by hiring foreign teachers, organising trips abroad, inviting foreign speakers and encouraging the girls to become pen friends with girls in other countries. The outbreak of war in 1939 involving so many of the major participants in the League had an obvious and disastrous effect on its work. Its activities dwindled away until it ceased operations entirely in 1946, its place in the international world taken by the United Nations, founded in San Francisco in 1945.

Keeping in Touch

Living in Wales again after her retirement, Connie rested. It took some time for her to regain her balance, but she stayed in touch. Her time as head of an independent girls' school may have been at an end, but her involvement with schools, universities, and similar educational institutions was far from over.

She remained closely connected to the UNIVERSITY COLLEGE OF WALES, Aberystwyth. During her headship of Dr. Williams' School, she had served as a member of the Council of the University and as an ex officio member of the Court. After her move to York, she remained a member of the Council, regularly attending meetings in Aberystwyth or London and contributing significantly to several of the special committees, notably those on student accommodations, finance, and building projects. As a member of the Council or of the Court she served Aberystwyth for the best part of thirty years.

After the death of her godson, Alexis, she set up travel scholarships for honours students or staff at "Aberystwyth, Manchester and York" in his name,[1] stipulating that in the case of the grants to Manchester and York the funds be used for travel to Russia or Greece (and by 1953 these had been taken up). In the case of Aberystwyth, she had stipulated Russia only, and this money had not been used. Surprisingly, in the spring of 1955, she was asked by the Principal of the College, Goronwy Rees,[2] if he might use the funds himself. There is no record of any reply from Connie, though she learnt subsequently that he did not in fact go to Russia. The funds were used instead by a member of the Department of Geology, Alan Wood, for a three-week trip. He was a member of a group of nine British scientists visiting science centres in Leningrad, Moscow, and Tbilisi to compare British and Soviet standards in science, as well as university teaching. The group concluded that the level was "much the same in both countries; that more interchange of ideas and travel between the two countries was needed; that many misconceptions on either side were corrected; and that exchange of staff and students between Soviet and British universities should lead to greater understanding." Much to Connie's satisfaction Wood added

1. SAUL, ECN to DR, March 1, 1946, and October 19, 1953, ms38515/5/96/4.
2. Goronwy Rees (1909–79) was a noted journalist and author, pre-WWII Marxist, member of MI6 (British intelligence), friend of Soviet agents Burgess and Maclean (and suspected of espionage himself), and Principal of University College Wales, Aberystwyth (1953–7).

that "your funding of the Alexis Aladin scholarship was timely and far-sighted" and that he much appreciated the grant he'd received: "Never have I learnt so much in three weeks."[3]

Her connection to DR. WILLIAMS' SCHOOL remained strong. She lived nearby, taught classes occasionally, and kept her cottage [Fig. 7.2] always open to Dr. Williams' girls and its Old Girls. When questions about the school's history were asked, she was amongst the first to be consulted. She took in hand, for example, a question asked in the summer of 1952.

Daniel Williams (1643–1716), whose legacy provided for the founding of the school, had in 1709 been awarded Doctor of Divinity degrees at Glasgow University and at the University of Edinburgh. Connie was asked to discover what had been said about him at the convocations conferring these degrees. On her behalf David Russell agreed to ask the secretaries of each university. Edinburgh replied only that the degree had been conferred in absentia. The Secretary of Glasgow University wrote that the Glasgow degree too was conferred in absentia, adding that the Faculty Minute gave no reason for it, since the reasons were well known: Williams was interested in the education of English Dissenters in Glasgow; he had provided already for the maintenance of several English students; and he had had conversations establishing a foundation for this purpose.[4]

She stayed close to the UNIVERSITY OF MANCHESTER too. While a student there she had lived in Ashburne Hall, and now she kept in touch with the Ashburne women by participating in several Ashburne committees, notably the Hostel committee, where she argued repeatedly for improvements. She also established a fund for travel scholarships for Ashburnian students and staff. What was most important was that, when considering a home for the large number of letters she had received from Alexis Aladin, it was the University of Manchester which came to mind. The letters, full of Aladin's political, social, and religious thoughts, most clearly reveal the state of mind of this Russian politician, soldier, and writer. Connie decided to give them to the university's John Rylands Library. Together with others of his papers, diaries, documents, newspaper clippings, and memorabilia of

---

3. SAUL, ECN to DR copy of letter from Alan Wood to ECN, October 13, 1955, ms38515/5/96/4.
4. By the terms of his will such a foundation was set up.

Fig. 7.2. *Ty Newydd in a recent photograph, with outbuildings converted by a subsequent owner. (Photo: Morris Higham; courtesy Morris Higham)*

all sorts in her possession, they arrived at the John Rylands in 1966, the year before she died. These materials had previously been examined in 1945 by Professor B. H. Sumner, who had proposed that the most informative should go to Cambridge University Library.[5]

At the MOUNT SCHOOL, YORK, as at Aberystwyth and Manchester, she set up travel scholarships. She also continued to take part in administrative meetings at the school and attended opening ceremonies whenever she could, most important of which to her may have been the dedication of a new science building in 1955. In the city she maintained her interest in the Settlement for Adult Education, which aimed to train working-class adults in citizenship (and of which she had once, while Head of The Mount School, been chair), and in the university, where many later recalled her

---

5. Professor Benedict Humphrey Sumner (1893–1951), Warden of All Souls College, Oxford was the most respected scholar of Russian History in Britain. A prolific author with a prodigious memory and a genial personality he was universally admired. Letter of May 20, 1945, John Rylands Library, Box 33.

membership in an early York University Planning Committee. Her interest in prison reform continued to take her to the open prison for women at Askham Grange, on the outskirts of the city, where she was a member of the management committee.

New Directions

A letter to David Russell in the St. Andrews University archives signals a new direction in Connie's life.[6] As education receded as her primary concern, she planned to give more time to the NATIONAL COUNCIL OF WOMEN and to the work of the UNITED NATIONS. It was not that she viewed the education of girls and the more general improvement of women's lives as competing objectives; rather, she saw them as complementary paths to fuller lives. She admitted that "at first" she hadn't believed in all of the Council's work, but she had come round to supporting its creed of "Better homes, Better moral standards and Better international relations" – ideals first outlined by the INTERNATIONAL COUNCIL OF WOMEN, the federation that linked the National Councils together. Though she supported the benefits brought by the welfare state, it would be, she wrote, "a sorry world" where there was no place for voluntary associations. The next decade of her life saw her working for the NCW and ICW, participating vigorously in conferences, seminars, and meetings, including of the NCW's Diamond Jubilee (1955) Committee, where a fundraising scheme she proposed was well received.

The United Nations

Her work for the United Nations, which she had joined after the collapse of the League of Nations, continued.[7] Many UN member or affiliate countries set up United Nations Associations (UNAs) to spread knowledge of the UN's principles – the promotion of international cooperation, peace, and human rights – and to publicise its activities. Connie became a member of the National Council of the UNA Wales, travelling regularly under

---

6. SAUL, ECN to DR, March 22, 1954, MS 38515/5/96/4.
7. Her interest in the League of Nations had flourished during her time in Constantinople and her years as Head of Dr. Williams' School.

arduous conditions from Dolgellau to attend its meetings in Cardiff. These were held in the imposing, if austere, "Temple of Health and Peace": a secular and architecturally eccentric structure of the 1930s. Described loosely as art deco in style, it offered a capacious conference hall, meeting rooms, and a council chamber.[8]

The high point of Connie's work for the UN came during World Refugee Year (WRY, 1959–60), when she served as President of the National Council of the UNA Wales, orchestrating activities throughout the principality, chairing meetings in Cardiff, and attending higher-level conferences in London. The World Refugee Year aimed to raise awareness of the plight of refugees around the world, not only in Europe and the Far East. In so doing "RESETTLEMENT" emerged as a major problem for decision makers, encouraging the willingness of refugees to go to a volunteer country or of a volunteer country to take in identified refugees. Such topics involved thorny conversations about refugees returning to their countries of origin or, with agreement on either side, being included in local populations. Bringing to these discussions her logical mind, calm disposition. and wealth of experience, Connie was in her element.

She would have been sharply reminded of the plight of refugees forty years earlier in Constantinople, when she herself had witnessed at first hand the abysmal conditions in refugee camps, the poverty of the physical shelter provided, the lack of hygiene, and the psychological despair. Similar conditions of despair and discomfort were still to be found in 1959–60, fifteen years after the end of World War II. A public relations campaign highlighted the work the UNHCR (United Nations High Commissioner for Refugees) had done in alleviating distress and settling refugees; it also took account of fundraising efforts launched in several countries, notably Germany, Austria, Britain, the United States, New Zealand, Australia, and the Scandinavian nations. By the mid-1960s the worst of the camps had been broken up and most of the refugees resettled, so that Connie could be satisfied with the work the WRY had set in motion and the part the National Council of the UNA Wales had played. All were aware, however, that new problem areas around the world were continually emerging.

---

8. Since 2018 it has been owned by Cardiff University.

National Council of Women

Founded in 1895 as the National Union of Women Workers, in 1897 the National Union affiliated with the International Council of Women, taking part that same year in the ICW's campaign "Equal Pay for Equal Work." Its objectives were clear enough. In 1918 its name was changed to the National Council of Women of Great Britain.

A service at St. Paul's Cathedral in 1955 marked the culmination of the National Council's Diamond Jubilee Year, in the fundraising for which Connie had so ably participated. Over the year the NCW had concentrated its efforts in two areas: the investigation of acts and policies that discriminated against women in every aspect of life, and the encouragement of women to speak up, not just privately but in public. It continued into the 1960s to be a platform for the debate of the inequities faced by women at home, in the family, and in the workplace; for the definition of issues; and for the drafting of proposals for governments to implement. In all these areas Connie's well thought out views and her eloquence stressed the importance of systems and organisation. The committees on which she served – the Executive Committee, the Committee on International and Commonwealth Relations, the Education Committee, and the Wales Regional Committee (of which she was President) – all benefitted from her deliberate speech, her quiet presence, and her sense of humour.

International Council of Women

Founded in 1888 by Susan B. Anthony and others to promote and protect women's rights around the world, the ICW's earliest aim was to establish a National Council of Women in every self-governing country, its earliest achievement the organisation of regular meetings of representatives of such National Councils to unify their intentions, emphasising better treatment of women, better relations between nations, and peace in the world.

National Councils, however, were slow to get going; the United States was the first to be established, followed by Canada, but only these two were active by the time of the first ICW gathering in 1893. Slow at first to champion the cause of WOMEN'S SUFFRAGE, the ICW concentrated on broadening its appeal to include "all women of light and learning," members of the professions, trade associations, labor groups, book clubs, religious groupings, and so on, as well as those politically minded. By the turn of the century, however, it was involved not only in issues of women's health, education, and workplace equality, but also in the contentious issue of voting rights.

The success of the ICW was due largely to the personality of its first President, Ishbel Hamilton-Gordon, Lady Aberdeen, wife of the Governor General of Canada. Though unversed in any kind of political activity she threw herself into the task with great fervor and persistence, successfully guiding the ICW from its first congress to 1936. World War II disrupted its activities, but by the time of Connie's intensified interest it had regained its balance and was expanding its activities globally.

The objectives of the ICW were essentially those suggested to its affiliate National Councils: better homes, moral standards, and international relations. In international settings these aims were more complex than those in narrower national scenarios: the cultures, customs, and mindsets of nations far apart geographically and developmentally could differ considerably from one another and, more tellingly, from the European and American cultures from which the ICW sprang. For the ICW, it was agreed that the promotion of peace between nations and the settlement of disputes by diplomacy were issues of paramount importance. As such they took centre stage at all its conferences. At the same time, social matters critical to women's day-to-day lives – housing, hygiene, cleanliness, women's legal position in marriage, inheritance, property rights, pay and conditions in the workplace – commanded continuous discussion. These issues varied, sometimes widely, from nation to nation. Underlying all these questions was the need for education, for easier access for women to schools and colleges, for the promotion of careers beyond teaching and nursing, for encouragement towards the professions, the law, accountancy, medicine. In all areas the ICW argued for equal treatment for women and men.

A committed advocate for worldwide peace, Connie was invited to join the ICW's Standing Committee on Peace and International Arbitration. As equally committed to improvements in every aspect of women's lives, she joined various committees of both ICW and NCW addressing social questions. In discharging her duties, she travelled to conferences in the United States and Canada, in Finland and Switzerland, in Persia and Turkey, and closer to home in Manchester and London. She travelled in all weathers and under all conditions, and towards the end of her life even in ill health. At an ICW meeting in London a few months before her death a colleague remarked how fragile she looked; but also how compelling her voice still was, firmly committed to "the cause of peace and disarmament" to the end.[9]

In all her work for these organisations, she continually urged the more visible presence of women in high places. She stressed the need for women of competence to speak out, to understand the operation of systems, and to recognise the centrality of executive power: access to money, the power to hire and fire, to promote or relegate, to distribute or withhold grants and fellowships. She reiterated that, in every avenue, women were the equals of men. The value of her work may be gathered from a tribute by the President of the ICW, Mrs. Mary Craig Schuller-McGeachy, who wrote of her "contributing much to discussion and action from the limitless resources of an erudite mind and an urbane and compassionate spirit."[10]

Personal Matters

Much of what we know of Connie's private life in this period is, as before, found in her correspondence with David Russell. And much again revolves around Alexis Aladin and his son. What was to be done about Aladin's papers and his literary legacy? How best could his political career be memorialised, and its importance recognised?

The death of young Alexis in early 1945 had brought back to Connie the memory of his father's death. It had simultaneously reminded her of the need for an assessment of Aladin senior's writings and arrangements for their safekeeping. Accordingly, in May of that year she had invited the Professor of Russian History at Oxford, B. H. Sumner, to go to Dolgellau to look through Aladin's papers. Sumner took up Connie's invitation, but his recommendation that important materials be sent to Cambridge Uni-

---

9. In these commitments Connie echoed her well-known contemporaries, the Oxford pacifists, Vera Brittain (1893–1970) and Winifred Holtby (1898–1935).
10. Cited by K. Olwen Rees in his remarks at ECN's memorial service at the Friends' Meeting House, Euston Road, London, on February 29, 1968; programme, p. 15.

versity Library was not followed up.[10] Though the burden of her work appeared overwhelming to her – "I feel so pressed for time that I do not seem to get down to much outside the daily round"[11] – in March of the following year she turned her attention once more to the question of Aladin's papers. At Aberystwyth she showed Aladin's "early life" letters to University President Tom Jones; he thought the letters publishable and encouraged her to ask Russell to write a foreword.

Despite Jones's positive appraisal, however, the project languished some six and a half years until revived in October 1953 by Russell,[12] who suggested publication in the *Rothmill Quarterly*.[13] Connie replied enthusiastically, reiterating her request that Russell write a preface.[14] In her letter Connie stressed the "noncontroversial nature" of Aladin's letters in this "age of extremes," adding, "when intolerance, hatred and misrepresentation are so rife, it is helpful to read something so free from prejudice." She is surprised that, of all the authors she has read on the 1917 Bolshevik Revolution, only Bernard Pares mentions Aladin and the Peasant Party. Almost a year later (August 2, 1954) Russell wrote that the *Quarterly*'s editor was ready to print the letters but was suggesting that a brief biographical note about Aladin be included. Russell added a query: Could Connie help with this? Progress remained slow. On November 2 she wrote apologising for the delay in returning her corrections. A month later Russell wrote that pressure of space had forced Aladin's piece to be held over to the next issue; but he did send along a proof of the biographical note including Connie's corrections. At last, on May 5, 1955, Connie wrote that she had in her hands a copy of the *Quarterly* with the first article describing Aladin's childhood. A second article appeared the following year.[15]

---

10. R. F. Christian, "Alexis Aladin, Trudovik Leader in the First Russian Duma: Materials for a Biography," *Oxford Slavonic Papers*, 21 (1988): 131–52; idem, *Alexis Aladin: The Tragedy of Exile* (Ottawa: Legas, 1999), p. 10.
11. SAUL, ECN to DR, January 7, 1946, ms38515/5/96/4.
12. SAUL, DR to ECN, October 7, 1953, ms38515/5/96/4.
13. The *Rothmill Quarterly* was the in-house publication of the Tullis Russell Company of Fife, Scotland, the family's prominent paper factory; the foreword for each issue was written by David Russell himself.
14. SAUL, ECN to DR, October 19, 1953, ms38515/5/96/4.
15. "A Childhood," *Rothmill Quarterly* 26 (1954–5) and 27 (1955–6).

Though many of the letters focused on Aladin and his family, they are peppered with discussion of a wide range of social, religious, and political topics: the value of school and most college examinations (unhelpful, according to both); the efficacy of nontraditional medicine, especially that of the Kellgren Institute; ignorance about the Greek Orthodox Church and the need for a brief popular book on its history; the weakness of academic and ecclesiastical leadership; telepathy, the summoning of the dead, spiritualism, and otherworldly experience; devolution of political power from Westminster to Wales and Scotland (much favoured by Connie); and the merits of parliamentary candidates. Of the candidates for the Merioneth seat in the election of May 1955, Connie comments wryly:

> Here in Merioneth we have a curious choice: a Liberal National sponsored by the Conservatives, a Liberal, a Labour and a Nationalist. The personalities of the first three are pretty mediocre whilst the fourth is a forceful speaker who can make out a case on such poor foundations of fact that he leaves his opponents speechless by the audacity of his claims! The usual theme is that "Welsh culture" has been ruined by English rule. It is useless to point out that Local Authorities can do much.[16]

Any disappointment Connie felt at the calibre of the candidates in the general election was offset by satisfaction that her eldest sister, Edith, was to receive an Honorary Master of Arts degree from the University of Manchester for services to education and health. The fact that she herself was free in July to travel to Manchester to attend the award ceremony made the anticipation of the day even more pleasurable.

By the mid-1950s the pace and variety of Connie's life had quickened appreciably, as her activities in a three-week period in 1955 show. After a summer holiday in Switzerland with her friend Melita Alexander and Melita's sister, Kathleen, we find her staying in London with the Alexanders again.[17] Somehow, the connection with Russia persisted. Going to Highgate on October 14 to have lunch with Kathleen Alexander, Connie's taxi

---

16. SAUL, ECN to DR, May 22, 1955, ms38515/5/96/4.
17. Melita Alexander, also a Quaker, had served for a time as Connie's secretary at The Mount School. Her brother, Sir Frank Alexander, Lord Mayor of London in 1944–5, was also a leading figure on the Baltic Exchange. The Alexanders often looked after Connie when she was in London.

was passed by cars full of Russian naval officers and their British hosts; she later discovered they had been on a pilgrimage to Karl Marx's grave. The following day (a Saturday) she and Melita went to the theatre; there, seated in front of them, were more Russians: ten naval officers and fifty other ranks, also with their British counterparts. On the Monday following, going to Church House, Westminster, for a committee meeting, there was a police motorcyclist directly behind her taxi leading the Lord Mayor's car and others with still more Russians – doctors who were staying at the Mansion House. She would have thought these encounters coincidences if Aladin had not always insisted that every incident in life has meaning. To top it off, the next day (the 18th) she learnt that one of her Mount School girls, Mary Ure, would be the first British actress to perform in the USSR since the revolution; she was going to Russia to play Ophelia.[18]

Returning to Dolgellau on the 24th, Connie paused for a day before going to Aberystwyth for a University Council meeting. While there, the University Principal, Goronwy Rees, told her that the Professor of Russian at Oxford, Sergei Konovalov, had mentioned the name of Alexis Aladin in conversation. Konovalov had become quite "excited," describing Aladin as "one of the best orators of Russia" and exclaiming that he had been trying to find out "what happened to Aladin after he came to England." Rees said he would ask Konovalov to write to her. Not knowing anything about Konovalov, Connie now wrote to Russell about him.[19] Three days later she was back home, preparing to leave on the cross-country journey to York; she had promised to be at The Mount School for the weekend of the 29th, when Lady Moberly[20] was to open the newly completed science block.

---

18. SAUL, ECN to DR, October 27, 1955, ms38515/5/96/4. The production starred Paul Scofield as Hamlet and was directed by Peter Brook; Alice Griffin, "Current Theatre Notes, 1955–1956," *Shakespeare Quarterly* 8.1 (1957): 71–89, at 74. Mary Ure was great niece of Sir Alexander Ure, Solicitor General for Scotland. Judi Dench, another of Connie's Mount School aspiring actress students, once – so family lore has it – exclaimed from the stage, theatrical award in hand, "Thank you, Miss Nightingale!"
19. SAUL, ECN to DR, October 27, 1955, ms38515/5/96/4.
20. Wife of Sir Walter Hamilton Moberly, Chair of the University Grants Committee 1935–49.

Replying to Connie about Konovalov,[21] Russell said he had asked a neighbor, a Mr. Higgs – a fluent Russian speaker and longtime resident in Russia who was due to be in Oxford shortly – if he would approach Konovalov, and Higgs had agreed to do so. But Connie, writing from London, declined to follow Russell's plan; she was already conferring with two other friends, also Oxford professors, who may have had other ideas. Nothing seems to have come of this promising initiative.[22]

On November 3, the very day Russell was writing to her, Connie was on her way to London again, this time for the memorial service for Tom Jones, who had died on October 15; she would stay, as so often, with the Alexanders. Immediately after the service – well attended by politicians, civil servants, and prominent academics – Connie returned to Dolgellau, a long and tiring journey for a woman of her age. She was in time to catch her breath (barely) before another visit to Aberystwyth on university business on the 5th. The endless moving about of these weeks gives a sense of what was important to her in her life's penultimate phase: she was constantly on the go.

Six months later Connie suffered another, more terrible loss: David Russell died unexpectedly. He had dictated a letter to Connie on May 11 with family news, intending to send with his letter the proofs of Part VI of Aladin's reminiscences, "A Childhood," due to be published soon in the *Rothmill Quarterly*.[23] A few days later his daughter wrote briefly to Connie saying that her father had died "very peacefully early on Saturday morning, but it was very sudden and naturally it has been a great shock especially to my mother." She included with her letter her father's dictated letter and the proofs he had intended to send, also mentioning the telegram sent earlier by the family and her father's obituary in *The Times*.[24] So ended the correspondence between two great friends first linked by their shared friendship with Alexis Aladin, the Russian exile they both had supported so liberally during his years of impoverishment in England.

21. SAUL, DR to ECN, October 31, 1955, ms38515/5/96/4.
22. SAUL, ECN to DR, November 3, 1955, ms38515/5/96/4.
23. SAUL, DR to ECN, May 11, 1956, ms38515/5/96/4. Written in six parts, "A Childhood" was published as two.
24. SAUL, Margaret Anne Oliphant Russell to ECN, May 14, 1956, ms38515/5/96/4.

Fig. 7.3. *Connie Nightingale and grandniece Lucy Nightingale in Scarborough in 1964. (Photo: Barry Nightingale [Connie's nephew, Tom's son, and Lucy's father]; courtesy Lucy [Nightingale] Chamberlain)*

As the final decade of Connie's life went forward, her energy levels inevitably faltered, and memory waned. She travelled abroad to ICW meetings less and less frequently, finally restricting her journeys, with few exceptions, to Aberystwyth and London, and it was in London that she attended her last NCW conference the year before her death. Some of her last days were spent in Ty Newydd, her cottage at the foot of Cader Idris, the mountain she admired so much, others in Glandwr Hall, a property owned by her brother Tom, which overlooked the Mawddach estuary. Comforted by the presence of family members [Fig. 7.3], the ebb and flow of the estuary on one side and the enfolding slopes of the hills on the other, Ellen Constance Nightingale died quietly on December 19, 1967.

 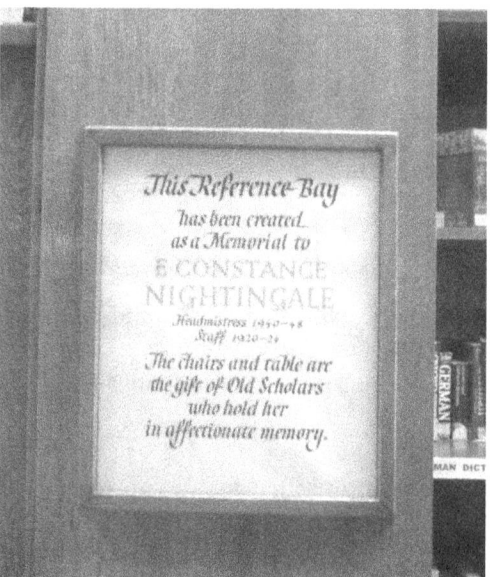

The Mount School library: bay, table, and chairs (left) and the tablet (right) recording the Old Girls Association's gift to the library in honour of Connie Nightingale, 1968. (Photos: Mary Pedley)

SELECT BIBLIOGRAPHY

Buchanan, George. *My Mission to Russia*, 2 vols. London and New York: Cassell & Co., 1923.
Christian, Reginald Frank. *Alexis Aladin: The Tragedy of Exile*. Ottawa: Legas, 1999.
Eames, Marion. Trans. Margaret Phillips. *The Secret Room*. Swansea: Davies, 1975.
Glasgow, George. *Ronald Burrows: A Memoir*. London: Nisbet & Co., 1924.
Jacob, Margaret C. *The First Knowledge Economy: Human Capital and the European Economy, 1750–1850*. Cambridge: Cambridge University Press, 2014.
London Committee of Unredeemed Greeks (G. Marchetti and others). *The Liberation of the Greek People in Turkey*. Manchester and London: Norbury, Natzio & Co., 1919.
Macintyre, Lorn. *Sir David Russell: A Biography*. Edinburgh: Canongate, 1994.
Macmillan, Margaret. *Paris 1919: Six Months That Changed the World*. New York: Random House, 2003.
Petsalis-Diomidis, Nikolaos. *Greece at the Paris Peace Conference (1919)*. Thessaloniki: Institute for Balkan Studies, 1978.
Scott, David Alexander. "Politics, Dissent and Quakerism in York, 1640–1700." Ph.D. diss., Dept. History, University of York, 1990.
Sheavyn, Brian. "Dr. Phoebe Sheavyn – Her History." 2007. Bound manuscript. National Library of Wales, Aberystwyth, Ceredigion. NLW ex 2599.
Sheavyn, Phoebe. *The Literary Profession in the Elizabethan Age*. Manchester: Manchester University Press, 1909; 2nd ed. revd. J. W. Saunders, 1967.
Sheils, Sarah. *Among Friends: The Story of The Mount School*, York: James & James, 2007.
Thistlethwaite, Frank. *A Lancashire Family Inheritance*. Cambridge: F. Thistlethwaite, 1996.
Tomos, Merfyn Wyn. *"Honour before Honours": The DWS Story*. Bala, Gwynedd, Wales: Nereus, 2009.

Archival Abbreviations
BIY   Borthwick Institute, York, Mount School Archive.
JRL   John Rylands Library, University of Manchester, Aladin Papers.
SAUL   St. Andrews University Library, David Russell Collection, files/records.

INDEX

Aberystwyth, *see* Wales, University College, Aberystwyth
Aladin, Alexis (Alec)
  career plans, 88–90
  childhood, 40, 43, 48–9, 50–1, 70–2, 76
  correspondence with Russell, 73, 74, 96
  death, 97, 99, 101
  ECN as godmother, 43, 44, 47, 51, 62, 105, 108
    adoption of, 63, 76–7
  education, 46, 49, 72–6, 89–91
  health, 46, 62, 72, 73, 96
  mother, *see* Spence, Florence
  and Russell family, 71, 75–6, 78, 96, 99
  travel scholarships in his name, 109–10, 111
  travels, with ECN, 74, 78
  and WWII, 89, 96–7; *see also* Royal Navy, Fleet Air Arm
Aladin, Alexis Feodorovich
  as Anglophile, 40, 42, 69
  childhood and education, 29–30
  death and estate, 47, 48, 62–3, 70, 76
  and ECN
    correspondence, 39, 40–8, 62, 82, 108
    financial support, 40, 43, 44, 45, 46–7, 48
    first meeting, 29, 35–7, 38, 107–8
    reputation tended, 69–70, 79, 100, 116, 119–20
  family, 29, 32, 40; *see also* Aladin, Alexis (Alec); Spence, Florence
  health, 46–7
  as journalist, 32–3, 40, 45, 70
  lectures, 32, 37
  literary legacy, 100, 116–18, 120
  and mysticism/religion, 28, 41–3, 46, 63, 70
  as orator, 31, 107, 119
  and Russell, 38, 42, 43, 47, 48, 99, 120
    financial support, 40, 43, 44, 45
  and Russia
    attempts to return, 32, 33–4, 69
    exiles, 30, 32, 43, 44, 45, 100n49, 107, 120

Aladin, Alexis Feodorovich *(cont,)*
  in First Duma, 30–2, 33, 69
  travel scholarships in his name, 100
  as soldier, 34–5, 69, 70
Alexander, Melita, 71, 78, 95–6, 118–19, 120
Ananieva, Elizaveta (Liza), Aladin and, 31, 32
Ancoats, *see* University Settlement
Anglicanism, *see* Church of England
Anstey, Florence, DWS Headmistress, 54, 56
Antigoni (Burgazada), Princes Islands, 26
Art and Crafts movement, 19, 65, 93
Ashburne Hall, University of Manchester, 13–14, 16–18, 110
Askham Grange, women's prison, 112
Atatürk, Mustafa Kemal, 27
Athens, 24, 25

Baldwin, Stanley, 100n46
Barmouth, Wales, 66, 68, 121
Barnsley, Edward, 65–6, 83, 93
Belgium, Aladin in, 30, 32
Board of Education, 64
  ECN and, 61n8, 79, 92
Bolsheviks, 34, 69, 117
Bootham School, York, 20, 21
  Alec at, 75–6, 89, 90
  and The Mount, 87–8, 94–5
Boothe [Luce], Clare, Aladin and, 40, 41
Braunholtz, Mary, 89n16
British Museum Library, 30, 43
Brookwood Cemetery, Surrey, 48
Bryn Mawr (Penn.), 58
  College, 15–16
Buchanan, George, 34
Burnley, Lancashire, 1–2, 5, 14, 17, 46, 106
  Grammar School, 8–10, 13, 105
Burrows, Ronald, 13, 17, 18, 23, 27, 106

Cader Idris (mountain), 54, 68, 71, 105, 121
Caernarfonshire, Wales, 60
Caernarvon (Caernarfon), Wales, 54
Calais, 36, 37

125

Cambridge University
  Library, 111
  Newnham College, 14
  Pembroke College, Alec and, 90–1, 96
  Trinity College, 38
Canada, 85, 96, 114, 115
  ECN in, 115
Catholicism, 53, 58
Chernyshevsky, Nikolai, 29–30
Church of England, 53, 58, 114, 118
Collcutt, Thomas Edward, 14
Conference on Russians Abroad, 45
Conservative Party (Tories), 12, 118
Constantinople, 21, 24–5, 26, 27, 36, 55, 101, 107, 113
  Ecumenical Patriarchate, 22
  Pera Palas Otel, 26
Cossacks, Aladin and, 34, 35, 43, 69
Cressbrook School, Kirkby Lonsdale, 73, 75
Cromarty Firth, Scotland, 97
Czechoslovakia, 43, 44, 84

Daily Express, Aladin and, 45
Dalton Hall, University of Manchester, 17, 21
Dench, Judi, 119n18
Denikin, Gen. Anton, 34, 35
Denisov, Gen. Svyatoslav, 24
Dissenters, 11, 53, 81, 110
Dolgellau, 68, 105
  ECN and, 44, 51, 116, 119, 120; *see also* Dr. Williams' School
  School Board, 54
Dorotheos, Patriarch of Constantinople, 27, 38
Dowson, Felix Needham, 73–4, 75
Dr. Williams' School [DWS], 100
  Alec and, 51, 62, 71, 76
  continental tours, 66
  ECN as Headmistress, 44, 45, 54–61, 64–9, 72, 78, 82–3, 85, 86, 106, 109
    and construction, 58–61, 64–6, 83–4, 93
    and music, 58, 66, 67–8, 93
    Wales featured, 59, 60, 67, 71, 86
  ECN as teacher emerita, 110
  former students, 44, 58n7, 64
    Old Girls Association, 56, 60, 61, 66, 110
  founding, 54
  Golden Jubilee (1928), 60, 61, 64, 66
  Junior School at Tremhyfryd, 59, 73
  Penycoed, senior girl quarters, 64
  see also Anstey, Florence
Dr. Williams's Library, London, 53
Dutton, Gladys, 57

Eames, Marion, 58n7
Earnseat School, Arnside, 73–4, 75
Edinburgh, 18n5, 96
  University of, 110
    Alec and, 90–1
Education Act, 53 (1870), 92 (1944)
Egypt, 42, 47, 94, 97
Eisteddfod (Welsh cultural festival), 59, 66–7
El Alamein, 94, 97
Ellis, Rowland, 58n7

English Dialect Dictionary, 16

Fairbourne, Wales, 66
Fife, Scotland, 90, 101
Fitch & Son, 42
Fox, George, 1, 58, 81
France, 24, 66, 84, 87–8, 99
  Aladin in, 30, 33
  see also specific locale
Friends of Russian Freedom, 37
Friends War Victims Relief Committee (later, Friends Relief Service), 25n11, 97–8

Germany, 84–5, 93; *see also* World War II
Gibbon, Vera, *see* Lowe, Vera (Gibbon)
Gimson, Sydney and Jeannie, 18, 19
  family, 18–19, 65n16, 93n30
Glandwr Hall (Tom Nightingale home), Barmouth, Wales, 121
Glasgow, 18n5
  University of, 110
Gold Cross of the Holy Sepulchre, 28, 107
Gorton, Rev. Neville, 73, 75–6
Grant, William Milner, and his school, 8
Gray, Donald, 75
Great Exhibition (1851), 12
Greco-Turkish War (1919–22), 25
Greece, 23–4, 109
  ECN and Alec travels, 74, 77–8
  refugees, 22–3, 25, 26–7
  see also Unredeemed Greeks
Greenwich Hospital (Conn.), 40

Haberdashers' Aske's School for Girls, London, 15
Hallé, [Sir] Charles, 13
Hamilton-Gordon, Ishbel, Lady Aberdeen, 115
Hampstead, 43, 46, 48–9
Harkness, Edward, 100n47
Harlech, Wales, 67, 100
Heraclitus, 44, 47
Herford, C. H., 14–15, 16
Holland, Samuel, 54
Howard de Walden, Thomas Scott-Ellis, 8th Baron, 65

International Council of Women (ICW), 112, 114–15, 121
  Standing Committee on Peace and International Arbitration, 115–16
Inverness, Scotland, 96
Iona, Scotland, 78, 96
Ireland, 53, 88
Istanbul, *see* Constantinople
Italy, 24, 36, 97, 99
  ECN in, 66, 78

Jewish refugees, at The Mount, 84
Jones, Thomas, 100, 117, 120

Kazan, University of, 30, 100n49
Kellgren, Jonas and Vera, 38

INDEX

Kerensky, Alexander, 30, 34, 41, 69, 70
Keynes, Maynard, 108
King's College London, 23
Kirkby Lonsdale, Westmorland, 73
Konovalov, Sergei, 31n2, 119–20
Kornilov, Gen. Lavr, and Aladin, 34, 69
Kurc, Marta, 84n9

Labour Party, 118
Lady Manners School, Bakewell, Derbyshire, 19, 106
League of Nations, 112
    DWS branch, 60, 66, 93, 108
    and ECN, 93, 108
Leicester, 14, 18, 19, 106
    School of Art, 19
    Secular Society (and Hall), 18–19
Lenin (Vladimir Ilyich Ulyanov), 30, 33, 41
    and Aladin, 30
Leningrad, 109; *see also* Saint Petersburg
Leslie and Nightingale (firm), 5–6
Liberal Party, 12, 44, 118
Lloyd George, David, 44, 100n46
Lloyd George, [Dame] Margaret, 44, 64
Lloyd George, Olwen Elizabeth, 44
London, 18n5, 19, 24, 51, 60
    Aladin in, 30, 32
    Committee of Unredeemed Greeks, 24, 106
    ECN in, 27–8, 37, 38, 45, 79, 101, 107, 109, 113, 116, 118–19, 120, 121
    National Liberal Club, 38, 43, 70
    Ritz Hotel, 38
    Russian Embassy, 32
    School of Slavonic and East European Studies, 89
    Sheavyn in, 14, 15, 16
    St. Paul's Cathedral, 114
    St. Thomas's Hospital, 46
    University, 92
        Birkbeck College, 14
Lowe, Vera (Gibbon), 55n3, 66, 67–8

MacLeod, Rev. George, 78, 96
Manchester, 1, 2, 3, 11–13, 18n5, 106, 116
    University of, 13
        ECN and, 10, 16, 19, 23, 54, 105–6, 110, 118; travel scholarship set up, 109, 110
        John Rylands Library, 12, 39, 108, 110–11
    see also Ashburne Hall; Dalton Hall
Manchester Guardian, 13, 48
Marx, Karl, 119
Mawddach River, 54, 68, 121
McConnell, James, 11
Mechanics Institutes, 4
Merioneth, Wales, 54, 60, 79, 118
Moonbeams Ltd., 32, 48
Moore, [Sir] Jonas, 2
Morning Post, Aladin and, 45, 48
Morris, William, 19
Mount School, The, York, 21, 43
    Board of Governance, 88, 92, 94, 95, 102
    and Bootham boys, 87–8, 94–5
    ECN and, 27, 38, 39, 54, 106, 119

Mount School, The, York (cont.)
    Headmistress, *frontis.*, 62, 64, 78, 82–8, 91–6, 97–8, 99, 100, 102, 106
    General Committee, 62, 79, 82, 84
    graduates, 92, 119
    Mount Magazine, 94–5
    Quaker origins and support, 82, 86
    travel scholarships set up, 109
    and WWII, 85, 86–8, 94, 97, 105
        aftermath, 97–8
        Cober Hill, 85–6, 95–6
        refugees, 84, 93
    see also Waller, Ellen C.

Nabokov, Vladimir, [Sr.], 32–3
National Council of Women (NCW), 112, 114, 115, 121
    Diamond Jubilee (1955), 112, 114
National Council of Unredeemed Greeks, 22, 106
National Trust, 19
    for Scotland, 97
Nightingale Bros., 6–7
Nightingale, Ellen Constance (Connie) [ECN]
    childhood, 1, 2, 4, 6–8, 106
    correspondence, *see* Aladin, Alexis Feodorovich, and ECN, correspondence; Russell, David, ECN correspondence
    death, 116, 121
    education, 2, 4, 8–10, 13–14, 17–18, 19, 105–6
    family, 4–8, 17, 121
        Alice (sister), 4, 26–7
        Annie (née Clitheroe; mother), 4, 6, 7–8, 10, 46, 78, 106
        Dora (sister), 4n4
        Edith (sister), 4, 6, 7–8, 10, 118
        Elizabeth (Beth; sister), 6, 7, 8
        Elizabeth (Betty; née Robinson; grandmother), 5
        Florence (sister), 4n4, 6, 7
        John (great-uncle), 7
        Kathleen (sister), 4, 7, 29, 36, 49, 50; *see also* Stedmond, Rev. Jock
        Luther (uncle), 6
        Marion (sister-in-law), 84n9
        Thomas (Tom; brother), 4, 7, 84n9, 106, 121
        Thomas (father), 4, 5, 6–7, 14
        Thomas (great-uncle), 4
        William (grandfather), 4–5, 6
        William (uncle), 6, 7, 10
    financial support of Florence and Alec, 48–9, 50
    Gold Cross of the Holy Sepulchre, 28, 107
    health, 19, 45–6, 47–8, 72, 99–100, 101–3, 105, 116, 121
    and mysticism/religion, 47; *see also* Quakers, ECN and
    retirement, 102–3, 108–9, 112–21; *see also* Ty Newydd
    as teacher/head, *see specific school*
Novoye Vremya (*New Times*), Aladin and, 33

Old Girls, *see* Dr. Williams' School, former students
Orient Express, 29, 36, 38
Oxford University, 16, 89, 92, 119–20
   Somerville College, 14, 16

Pankhurst, Emily, 12
Pares, [Sir] Bernard, 70, 96, 117
Paris
   Aladin and, 45
   DWS tour, 66
   ECN and, 36, 37, 40, 75, 106
Paris Peace Conference (1919–20), ECN and, 20, 21–4, 26, 27, 54, 106–7
Parliament, British, 4, 53
Paterson, Basil, 90
Peasant Party (Trudoviks), 31, 69, 107, 117
Penrose, Emily, 14, 16
Persia, ECN in, 115
Poland, 66, 84
Popov, Gen. Iosif, 24
Prague, 43–4
Presbyterians, 38
Proodos (*Progress*), 24–5, 54, 107

Quakers
   early, 1, 58, 81, 84
   ECN and, 17, 20, 21, 25n11, 42, 58, 65n16, 79, 82, 106, 118n17
   schools, *see* Bootham School; Mount School
   see also Friends War Victims Relief Committee
Quest Society, 42, 99

Rees, Goronwy, 109, 119
Rothmill Quarterly, 117, 120
Rowe, J. W. F., 90–1
Royal Academy Exhibition, 46
Royal Navy
   Alec and, 97
   Fleet Air Arm, 89, 91, 96, 97n38
   Women's Royal Naval Service (WRNS), 98
Russell, [Sir] David
   death, 120
   ECN correspondence, 4, 25, 61n8, 85, 96, 100–1, 112, 119–20
      on Aladin, 62–3, 69, 70, 103, 116–17
      on Alec, 49–50, 51, 62–3, 69, 70–7, 88–90, 96, 99, 103
      on health, 26, 101–3
      on Russell and family, 98–9
   family
      Alison (wife), 75, 78, 97, 120
      David Francis Oliphant (son), 72, 73, 75, 97, 99
      fondness for Alec, 71, 75–6, 96
      Margaret Anne Oliphant (Anne; daughter), 99, 101, 120
      Patrick (son), 72–3, 75, 97, 99
   financial support of Florence and/or Alec, 48–9, 71, 96
   friendship with Aladin, 37, 49, 99, 120
   homes, 90, 96, 101
   and Iona, 78

Russell, [Sir] David *(cont.)*
   knighthood, 99
   and publication of Aladin letters, 100, 117–18, 120
Russia
   British Embassy, 70
   ECN and, 38–9, 79, 100, 108, 109, 118–19
   Mount School and, 109, 119
   Provisional Government, 30
      Aladin and, 34, 69, 108
   Social Democratic Labour Party, 30
   see also specific locale; Soviet Union
Rylands, John and Enriqueta, 12

Saint Petersburg, 30, 32, 33; *see also* Leningrad
Schuller-McGeachy, Mary Craig, 116
Scotland
   Aladin in, 42, 47
   Alec in, 71, 75–6, 96
   ECN and, 4, 78, 101, 118
   see also specific locale
Scott, C. P., 13
Sedbergh School, Yorkshire, 73
Sheavyn, Phoebe, 14–16, 18, 106
Sidgwick, Eleanor, 13
Sidgwick, Henry, 38
Simbirsk, 30–1, 32
Smith, Gaynor (Williams), 55n4, 56n5
Society for Cultural Relations, 108
Society for Psychical Research, 38
Society of Friends, *see* Quakers
Southampton, 48, 49, 50
Soviet Union (USSR), 108–9, 119; *see also* Russia
Spanoudi, Sophia, 25
Spanoudi[s], Ninitza, 25–6
Spanoudis, Alexander, 26
Spanoudis, Konstantinos, 24–5, 106–7
Spence, Florence, 40, 44, 62
   employment, 48, 51, 63, 71
   evaluated by Stedmond, 50–1
   supported financially, 43, 48–9, 50, 76
St. Andrews, University of, 40, 43, 100
   archives, 98, 112
Stedmond, Doreen, 50
Stedmond, Kathleen, *see* Nightingale, Kathleen
Stedmond, Rev. Jock, housing of Alec and Florence, 49, 50, 71
Stoneywell Cottage, Gimson home, 18, 19
Sumner, Benedict Humphrey, 111, 116–17
Sweden, 38, 66
Switzerland, ECN in, 115, 118

Thornber, B., and Sons, textiles, 3
Thornber, Sharp, 5, 8, 10
Times, London, 48, 120
Treaty of Lausanne, 27
Treaty of Sèvres, 27, 38
Treaty of Versailles, 21, 26
Trieste, 29, 36
Tudor Pole, Wellesley, 42, 49, 50
Tuke, Esther and William, 81–2
Tuke, Samuel, 82

Turkey, 22–3, 25, 27, 106
  ECN in, 115
Ty Hyfryd, 71–2
Ty Newydd, ECN cottage, 55, 71–2, 102, 105, 110, 121

Unitarians, 11, 12
United Nations, 108
  ECN and, 112
  High Commissioner for Refugees, 113
  UNA Wales, 112–13
United States, 40–1, 66, 114
  Aladin and, 32, 44
  ECN and, 7, 10, 15–16, 100, 115
University Settlement, Ancoats, 17, 23, 106
Unredeemed Greeks, 22, 24, 28, 106
Ure, Mary, 119

Vaughan, Robert Alfred, 47
Venice, ECN and, 36, 37
Venizelos, Eleftherios, 24, 106

Wales, 53, 58, 67
  and Quakers, 58
  ECN affection for, 59, 60, 71, 78–9, 83, 118
  cottage in, *see* Ty Newydd
  North, 54, 85
  University College, Aberystwyth, 14, 16, 67, 100, 109, 117, 120, 121
    Council, ECN on, 79, 100, 109, 119
    Court, ECN on, 78, 109
    travel scholarship set up, 100, 109–10

Wales *(cont.)*
  University College, Cardiff, 13
  see also specific locale; Eisteddfod
Waller, Ellen C., Headmistress, The Mount, 79, 82, 84
Watt, James (actuary), 77
Watt, James (inventor), 11
Westminster, 32, 79, 118, 119
Westmorland, 73
White Army, 35, 69, 107
Williams, Daniel, DWS namesake, 53, 110
Women's Franchise League, 12
Women's Social and Political Union, 12
Wood, Alan, 109–10
World Refugee Year (1959–60), 113
World War I [WWI], 2, 24, 85, 106
  and education, 19–20, 79
World War II [WWII], 3, 84–5, 86, 87–8, 97, 108, 113, 115
Wrangel, Gen. Pyotr, 35
Wrexham, Wales, 53

Yegorov, M. E., 33
York
  Adult School, 85
  ECN and, 21, 79, 109; *see also* Bootham School; Mount School
  Settlement for Adult Education, 111
  University Planning Committee, ECN on, 112
  WWII and, 85–7, 93–4, 97

Zon, Raphael, 100

www.ingramcontent.com/pod-product-compliance
Lightning Source LLC
Chambersburg PA
CBHW051212290426
44109CB00021B/2426